Design by Sigmar Berg

Cover photography by Gerhard Merzeder

Printed in the United States of America

First Printing, 2023

ISBN-13: 978-1-960583-73-4 hardcover edition

ISBN-13: 978-1-960583-74-1 paperback edition

ISBN-13: 978-1-960583-75-8 e-book edition

Waterside Productions

2055 Oxford Ave

Cardiff, CA 92007

www.waterside.com

BREATHE I BE PRESENT I INVITE LOVE

one journey®

THE LOVETUNER BOOK

BY SIGMAR BERG

WITH ANNE WOLNIK

DISCLAIMER

The information included in this book is general information and should not be used to diagnose or treat a health problem or disease. Do not use this information as a substitute for professional health care advice.

Lovetuner, Sigmar Berg, and Anne Wolnik do not make any representation or warranty (expressed or implied) contained in, or for any omissions from, the information on this page. This disclaimer of liability applies to any damages or injury whether based upon consumer law, negligence, or any other cause of action.

By partaking in any of the exercises herein, such as but not limited to, Lovetuner tuning (including meditation) that are offered by Lovetuner, the participant takes complete responsibility for their safety, health, and overall physical, emotional, and mental well-being.

All source references, bibliographical references, and graphic references in this document have been noted to the best of our knowledge and belief. Misprints and errors are reserved.

TABLE OF CONTENTS

FOREWORD

BY GABRIELLA DE LA GARZA
ACTRESS AND ACTIVIST

One Journey describes the impressive spiritual path of Sigmar Berg, the founder of Lovetuner. In an easy-to-understand way, this book invites us to face the big questions of life.

Using Sigmar Berg's own example, the reader is enlightened about difficulties on the spiritual path and introduced to possible solutions.

It becomes clear that Lovetuner is much more than a product. Lovetuner is a global mission for peace and love.

The connection of all hearts on a global level is the basic prerequisite for peace on earth. Peace in this world comes when we create peace within ourselves.

The Lovetuner book takes the reader on a journey to oneself and shows comprehensible ways to self-empowerment.

The concrete exercise instructions are clear guides to raising one's consciousness and frequency to the magical frequency of 528 Hz, the vibration of love.

Each and every one of us can achieve unconditional love with the help of the Lovetuner by raising our own frequency, and thus making our contribution to spreading the frequency of love on our planet.

Love is the most powerful force in the universe and simply cancels all lower motivations. This will create a true global community where humanity lives as creation intended for us: free.

A philanthropic and encouraging spiritual book.

FOREWORD

BY SUZY BATIZ
ENTREPRENEUR AND PHILANTHROPIST

Sigmar Berg's One Journey: The Lovetuner Book is an enchanting invitation to awaken the symphony within and embrace the power of love. I am honored to share my hearts reflection on this profound journey of self-discovery.

From the first note, Sigmar's words strike a chord deep within, urging us to explore our inner landscape and resonate with our most authentic selves. With each turn of the page, we're led on a harmonious voyage, learning to breathe life into the Lovetuner that lies in the depths of our hearts. This book is a beacon of light, illuminating the path to self-love, connection, and the awakening of our souls.

As we journey through the chapters, Sigmar masterfully reveals the transformative power of the Lovetuner, a celestial instrument that can align us with the universe's divine frequency. By attuning to this vibration, we open our hearts and minds to the boundless possibilities that life has to offer. We learn to see the beauty in every moment, to embrace the magic of synchronicity, and to dance with the flow of life's ever-changing rhythm.

Through personal anecdotes, inspiring stories, and soulful insights, The Lovetuner Book transcends the boundaries of traditional self-help literature. It becomes a living, breathing guide that awakens our spirits and invites us to join a global chorus of love. As we tune into our hearts and harmonize with the Lovetuner, we discover a newfound sense of peace, joy, and belonging that reverberates through every facet of our lives.

In the spirit of love, I invite you to embark on this transformational journey and let the Lovetuner be your guide. Together, we can create a world where hearts sing in unison and love is the melody that connects us all.

FOREWORD
BY ADAM HALL
BEST SELLING AUTHOR AND FUTURIST

This captivating book possesses an extraordinary ability to metamorphose and elucidate love in every facet of your life.

Sigmar Berg's One Journey: The Lovetuner Book, ingeniously interweaves science and spirituality in a manner that is both easily accessible and deeply enlightening. While there are many tools on the path to love, only one can evoke a profound sense of serenity: the Lovetuner.

For the past five years, my partner and I have utilized the Lovetuner in myriad ways. On one occasion, we bestowed the Tuner upon our friends Sherie and Trolls, who were grappling with a crossroads in their 25-yearlong marriage. Uncertain whether to part ways or remain stuck, they began to tune and discovered a radical newness to their relationship, causing their love to once again blossom.

During another challenging time in my own relationship, when communication had faltered and I was adrift and bewildered, I began to tune. Remarkably, my anxiety and stress levels plummeted. When we subsequently tuned together, we shared laughter and a deep connection.

I have realized that the heart is the most powerful tool at our disposal, and what humanity needs most is a means to attune ourselves to its frequency. Similar to the restorative power of nature, the Lovetuner aids in regenerating the body, heart, mind, and soul. Ultimately, families and friends who tune together, stay together.

If you're looking to transmute fear into courage, hate into love, and create harmony in a world that appears to be in a state of chaos, look no further than this book. It will assist you in attuning your life to a frequency of peace, love, and abundance.

CHAPTER I

ONE JOURNEY

When I started writing this book, I was out on my ranch hugging a tree. Now you might be thinking I am some crazy hippy guy from California who hugs trees. Before starting this journey, I had the same thought about people who hugged trees, probably just some hippies with their heads too far up in the clouds.

It's not about hugging trees. Instead, I want to convey to you in this book my journey into the light—coming from the light, bringing the light, and returning to the light. Hugging a tree sounds very hippiesque, but it's not. It is what our universe and life are about, and that is frequency and vibration. When your physical, mental, and spiritual body is truly tuned in, you can embrace the vibration of a tree. At that moment you understand the universe.

The 528 Hz frequency resonates at the core of all living matter, so when you use the Lovetuner, you are tapping into that connection with nature. You are entering into resonance and communication with the natural planet. A similar experience occurs for people who take mushrooms, but what makes the Lovetuner so special is that you are creating this connection with your own exhale.

So when I talk about hugging a tree, it is not because I am a hippy with a love for trees. It is because I want to make this deep reconnection to nature available to everyone, and show people how through the discovery of our purpose in this creation we can create a harmonious world, overcoming superficial barriers that have been fabricated to cause polarity, disunity, and hostility.

You can use a very simple tool that has the power to connect you to this very feeling I'm talking about, where you see yourself at one point hugging a tree, connecting to the Source, connecting to Mother Earth, and just being a part of it. Recognize your frequency, raise your vibration, and come into resonance with your core frequency. It will allow you to attract better experiences as you leave the low-frequency level, and all that is associated with it.

Throughout this book, there might be moments when you think to yourself this is crazy. But I encourage you to follow me on this path and embrace a deep reflection into yourself, the world around you, and the search for life's purpose. This book will give you the essence of what it is and what it's all about, no matter where you are in life, no matter where you are going. This is a book for anyone brave enough to look into their own heart and understand the longing of their heart.

This goes beyond the comfort zones that have been created. To help the planet and humanity, one must first and foremost have a full understanding of what is going on.

To truly understand and comprehend what is going on in our world on a 5D level, you must leave your comfort zone. Currently, the majority of us live in a comfort zone, within the construct of the 3D world, what we might refer to as the Matrix. We have accepted superficial living, allowing others to dictate our lives, not searching for a true purpose. The Maslow's Pyramid states that one cannot progress to the next level of the pyramid, much less reach the top, until one fulfills the level below. At the bottom of this pyramid are the basic life necessities, food, shelter, etc. If you are kept occupied by fighting for basic survival needs, a life experience is wasted on just trying to stay alive. In this scramble for the shallow necessities of living, there is no room to explore spirituality and explore a meaningful purpose to your existence. We need to become aware of the constructed comfort zones we are living in and be willing to leave them behind if we ever want to spark change. As Neale Donald Walsch wrote, "Life begins at the end of your comfort zone."

Everything in the universe is connected to us, and change starts within ourselves—within our hearts. True experience creates the change that starts from within.

The Lovetuner is a divine creation. At one point, it just reminded me to look into my own heart and start doing what I was born to do.

The essence of what I learned on this journey started a long time ago, but physically this experience started a few years ago, and I want to be your facilitator with this tool. It has nothing or maybe everything to do with myself, but it is simply the best thing you can ever do for yourself, no matter what, because we all need to get from our head to our heart.

Like an oxygen mask on an airplane, you reach out and put it on yourself before you can help anyone else—that's exactly what the Lovetuner will do for you. It awakens your key to life.

Sigmar Berg, Lovetuner Founder

On How to Use the Lovetuner

Some of you already have a Lovetuner, and I want to encourage you to use your Lovetuner and tune in with me right now.

No matter where in the world you are, and whatever is going on in your life right now, is of no essence. It is only about you at this moment, in the here and now.

Take your Lovetuner and connect your exhale to the power of the 528 Hz frequency.

Let us all connect in this universal divine field of the 528 Hz love frequency.

Tune into your heart and feel the unity of all hearts connected to the universe.

All is one and one is all.

As we all need to get out of our heads and back into our hearts, I would love to invite you to the following heart coherence Lovetuner breathing exercise:

Here is a short introduction on how to use the Lovetuner; if you are already familiar with it, just jump right into it.

How to Tune:

1. Pull the Lovetuner out of the cap and place the side with the engraved Lovetuner logo between your lips.
2. Start with a deep inhale through the nose and gently breathe out through the mouth, which will create a subtle, audible tone, turning your exhale into the vibrational love frequency of 528 Hz.
3. Repeat a minimum of six times for an aligning effect. Repeat breathing cycles as often as needed. Repetitive tuning creates a more peaceful, calm, mindful, and aligned state of being.

After tuning, enjoy the silence and a harmonious aligned state of being. You can tune anywhere: at home, during office breaks, in the car, with friends, on your yoga mat, in nature, etc.

Having said this, I now want to invite you to our practical tuning and breathing exercise:

Put your Lovetuner between your lips, breathe in through your nose, and start to produce a soft, even tone as you exhale. Focus your attention on the soles of your feet. Imagine that you are deeply and firmly rooted in Mother Earth. Just let go of everything that has been bothering you. Nothing matters anymore, just you in the here and now at this moment.

We are going to tune six breathing cycles.

First, focus on your heart center. If you want, you can put your hands loosely on your heart.

While you inhale, you breathe light into your heart, and while you exhale, you breathe love out through your heart.

Now take the following positive thoughts, feelings, and images into your consciousness and send them beyond your heart field into everything around you while we are tuning together:

"I AM LOVE", we tune six breathing cycles.
"I AM GRATEFUL", we tune six breathing cycles.
"I AM PRECIOUS", we tune six breathing cycles.
"I AM HAPPY", we tune six breathing cycles.
"I AM FREE", we tune six breathing cycles.
"I AM HEALTHY", we tune six breathing cycles.

Let this wonderful vibration resonate in you for a while, and then come back slowly and consciously. Regardless of any prior education or interest in spirituality, with this simple exercise, we are all just connected to the web of love that embraces our world. Thank you for tuning with me and sharing your love with the world.

CHAPTER II

HEART COHERENCE

Allow me to give you some interesting facts about the Lovetuner and heart coherence.

In simple terms, heart coherence means the communication and unity of the heart and brain. As a result, breathing, heart-beat, and blood pressure are coordinated and work together healthily. These three areas and their interactions are considered to be of great importance to our overall well-being and have a strong influence on our physiological and psychological health.

Heart coherence enables us to use our resources optimally in everyday life as well as in professional situations. We are flexible, efficient, imaginative, and creative, and, therefore, positively influence our emotions and control them or deal with them better. This increases our resilience, which equates to psychological resistance or the ability to survive difficult life situations without lasting impairment.

Here is more insight into the meaning and philosophy of creating heart coherence by tuning with the Lovetuner. The latest scientific findings show that disorders in the interaction between the nervous system, heart, and brain can cause diseases such as stress, anxiety, depression, and burnout. Emotions and physical symptoms are related.

It is crucial for the development of diseases that essential parts of our body physiology (blood pressure, heartbeat, immune system, digestion, hormones, etc.) are not controlled by the neocortex but by the limbic system.

The limbic system is where our emotions are located in our brain and are biogenetically older than the neocortex, which is responsible for our logical thinking and consciousness. Therefore, our limbic system can take control of our neocortex without our consciousness being able to escape this influence. However, the influence of the neocortex on the limbic system is limited. It means that we can control our emotions much less directly than, for example, our motor functions. Thus, it does not help to give the logical command to not be afraid or to get excited in an anxious or stressful situation.

For example, a spider's sight can lead to a panicky escape reaction if the sight of a spider is filled with excessive negative emotions in the limbic system. It is useless if the affected person realizes that there is no danger objectively—the fear remains. This means that the part of the brain where our emotions are housed also controls essential bodily processes simultaneously, without our consciousness having direct control over them.

This is precisely why chronic overloading (chronic stress) and mental illnesses such as depression or fear make us physically ill. With these illnesses, the regulation of critical bodily functions deteriorates at the same time.

Heart Rythm Patterns

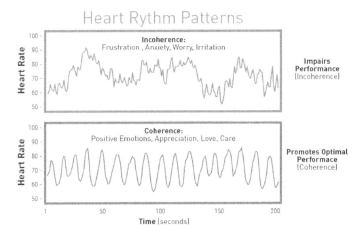

Heart coherence is the key to the limbic system and improved bodily functions. The limbic system can be best and most easily achieved by physical measures. A recognized method is heart coherence.

Here is more insight into the heart coherence exercise:

In the Lovetuner breathing exercise, you bring your attention to your heart center. With your heart focus, you create the opportunity to actively generate heart coherence with the help of your Lovetuner. By breathing through your heart with your Lovetuner, you activate the 528 Hz universal love frequency in each of your 37 trillion body cells, emitting light in the form of biophotons. Heart coherence means optimizing the synchronization of heartbeat, breathing, and blood pressure. Through this exercise, we learn to avoid stress and consciously generate relaxation. In this way, we consciously create mindfulness and high awareness.

We cannot influence our limbic system—our emotional center—through logical thinking. It can only be done by actively changing emotions. The regular establishment of heart coherence consequently means we do not let our system get into a tense state in the first place.

In this way, we bring joy, empathy, better communication, and ultimately peace and health into our lives.

Recent research also shows that heart coherence causes our system to produce more immunoglobulin A, an essential protein component of our immune system that forms an important protective barrier against viruses, bacteria, and fungi, especially during this time. As a positive consequence, a high-vibrational field means a robust immune system.

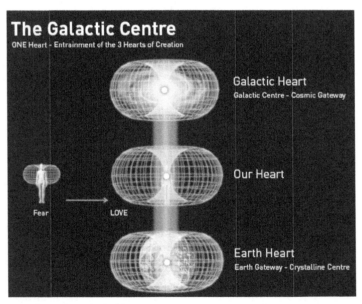

The Heart Magnetic Field

According to today's energetic medicine findings, the heart center is located in the middle of the chest at the heart level. It represents the spiritual center of love, our feelings, and emotions. Our heart functions like a radio station, and the 528 Hz frequency serves as a carrier wave onto which we project the desired information. Thus, through our sincere intention, we activate and emit feelings of love, gratitude, appreciation, health, freedom, etc., when we breathe in and out through our hearts.

CHAPTER III

IN THE BEGINNING

Why is it so important for me to share the knowledge behind this magical tool, the Lovetuner, with you?

On my journey to find out what this ancient solfeggio frequency is all about, I met people from various fields, different cultures and belief systems.

My first conscious connection to nature even then made me feel that there was something bigger out there, something more exciting because what we see is just the vibration that comes from nature. So, the earliest experience I can remember was when I was only a few years old, I had the first feelings of understanding the power of nature and our connection to it. At that time, I lived with my young parents at a lake in the

Salzkammergut in Austria. In the Salzkammergut, landscape, culture, and the love of tradition come together most beautifully. Writers, artists, and emperors were drawn to its shores early on. Mondsee Lake is a beautiful alpine lake surrounded by towering mountains also referred to as the Dragon Wall, which create a mystical feeling as they loom over the area. A powerful feeling lies between the contrast of the deep alpine lake and the tall mountains; it is a place where you recognize the strength and beauty that nature contains. As a young boy, I had an inexplicable feeling that being in this scenery, and not just admiring but recognizing the power of nature, is vital to my life. It made me aware of how big our planet is and that I am a part of this universe, a part of nature that I was admiring. This feeling has evolved throughout my life and it boils down to the understanding that while we might be a small part of this world and something bigger put us in this creation, we are all connected and have a purpose to fulfill beyond just accepting our existence. These thoughts as I express them now were not clear to me as a young boy, but looking back, it was one of those moments when you feel and understand the meaning of your journey.

To this day I still have vivid imagery of this lake in my mind. Those are the things that your heart embraces and holds that memory on a cellular level: whatever you do in your life, it's there forever.

One has the choice to never look at their role in this creation, but it is the understanding of creation and the understanding that each of us is a creator that helps you to define your purpose. As we are a part of the creation, yet at the same time we are creators so our actions have an impact. We are a part of the collective so whether your action is physical, mental, or spiritual, it has an impact. That is why it is so important to find your resonance because all your actions are in resonance with you. So if you tap into negativity, you are exposed to everything that resonates at that frequency. If you understand this, it is clear that you cannot retract yourself from life, because you only receive back what you put out.

Each of us has those moments when we receive precise messages about whatever event—funny or dramatic—or just random, as I described earlier. We often want to stay in our comfort zone and follow that very clear message. One of the first real visions I experienced happened to me in 1990 in Venezuela.

Sigmar, Puerto de la Cruz, El Morro, Venezuela 1990

Staring out over the ocean, shivering in the night for a glimpse in time, I saw a rich green maze from a bird's-eye perspective. In my vision, I watched from above, myself in the maze figuring out how to exit the maze. Usually, when you are in a maze, you are searching for the correct path out. You don't view each path as part of a great whole because you cannot see how the entire maze connects. I was able to see where we started and where it is that we need to go. This vision opened my eyes to the collective we are all a part of. It made me understand the microcosm and the macrocosm, us and the universe.

Little did I know back then that this evident and precise vision of being on a guided path in life would become my mission to share with the world at one point.

As the years passed, this clear message remained in my consciousness, even as I was distracted by daily life, struggling with whatever life was throwing at me or being too busy having fun.

Sigmar and his son Luis, Tarifa, Spain 2005

Becoming a father was the first big reminder of what life is all about and what my place at this particular time in my life needed to be. Bringing life into this world is one of the most purposeful experiences a human can go through. There are events within a lifetime that one should experience to become a whole person. One of those experiences for me was getting children. Becoming a father was the end of one chapter in my life and brought me to the next stage of my life. Up to that point, I had no responsibility for anyone else. I was living free and for myself; it was a very egocentric lifestyle. Once you have kids, that changes because they are a part of you, it is what you created. They are not someone you meet and spend time with—it shows you what it means to have responsibility. That is why it is so sad that people forget the responsibility that comes with creating life. Having children is the perfect reflection of our role in this creation, that we too are creators who add and give to this world. It is also a gift because when children enter your life they are bringing you to the next step of your journey.

Up to this point, I have lived my spirituality quietly, constantly feeling that something greater than life is waiting for me and worth revealing, and that it is my calling to share it with the world. I first learned about the 528 Hz frequency through Robin Clement during a 528 Hz sound and breathing meditation. Furthermore, this guided meditation combined with the 528 Hz frequency was the most profound meditation I'd experienced at the time, having meditated daily for years. It also immediately reconnected me with what I had seen for a short moment 23 years earlier.

The same clear image from Venezuela reappeared 23 years later.

Everything fell into place experiencing and sharing my deepest inner beliefs about what can heal the world. As I thought about healing the world, I realized that this could be the ultimate help for self-healing and self-empowerment.

A few weeks later, I met up with Tom Rohner, an old friend who had previously introduced me to Robin Clement, as they had already experimented with a tuner tuned to 528 Hz. Rest in peace, Tom.

Sigmar and Tom, Santa Monica, California 2014

Since their project was going nowhere, within two days I decided to take it over and create a high-quality product at a reasonable price that everyone could afford. At the time, I lived a very busy professional life as an international fashion designer and artist in Los Angeles.

From the first day, after I made this decision, I dedicated my passion and most of my time to this beautiful mission of love. Although my friends had gathered some feedback about the device and the basic knowledge about the 528 Hz frequency, the so-called love frequency, we entered an unknown territory but firmly believed that the Lovetuner, as a connector to this frequency, would show us the way, regardless of the lack of information.

Since it is impossible for the Lovetuner to be connected to anger, fear, greed, a sense of entitlement, or selfishness, I had no choice but to take on the mission and cut ties with everyone connected to these emotions.

This may sound harsh, but it is the truth. In this book, I want to make you aware that truth and authenticity are not even an option but a must to raise your frequency and live your life to the fullest.

Everything is frequency and vibration; you are sending out unambiguous signals and receiving very clear signals. The only thing that can hold you back is being out of tune. A musical instrument that needs to be tuned does not sound right. When you think of long, draining days, you usually feel out of tune and not in resonance with yourself. This causes you to do unfulfilling, purposeless things, such as surrounding yourself with people who have a low vibration and having relationships that do not bring out the best in you.

528hz

What I'm saying is that no one else can be held responsible for your signal and vibration, so you can determine for yourself what you tune into.

You will naturally be more in tune with higher frequencies by raising your frequency. However, if you are unaware of this and are in an ego state of mind, you will connect to lower frequencies.

You will find your core resonance, happiness, and purpose when you go into your heart. In the state of heart, you are fully aware of what you want and can manifest it. It's like tuning into your favorite radio station—you have to tune into the receiver to receive a clear signal.

CHAPTER IV

INSIDE JOURNEY

I would like to address something that I call the grey field of mixed messages.

You know what is good for you but do not want to change anything. Or you get messages that are just unclear because you are not in tune with yourself and the world around you. This is leading you into living an unauthentic life.

There is no societal restriction, no family or political constraint withholding you from tuning into this authentic feeling coming from your heart. This puts you in the position of getting an alert from your heart towards everything that is not in resonance with you. Learning to listen to the messages of your heart will enable you to eliminate all inauthenticity in and around you.

Authenticity is the key to living your life to the fullest. When out of tune, knowing what is good or bad for you is impossible. You are not tuned into the right frequency, not willing to tune into the right frequency, and listening to the wrong frequencies. You feel like you are a moving target and can only react to whatever comes your way. You are not in charge and are in victim mode. On the other hand, when you are in tune your senses are connected to your intuition, your actions are on time, and you are in the creator mode.

Often, I witnessed people looking for a shortcut and a quick fix and only focusing on the outside, getting frustrated and losing their ability to listen to their inner voice. It is like climbing up a ladder for years and years and finally figuring out that you've spent all this time climbing up the wrong ladder.

In life, you always have two choices: one is to refuse to change and stay with your old habits.

The other option is to change directions, change your behavior, and create a blank canvas for new experiences and spiritual growth. There is no shortcut to enlightenment. First, you have to face the facts and trust your gut feeling. By following your heart wherever you go, you call in spiritual guidance and get used to living your life being guided by higher consciousness. If you become aware of this, then you are ready to connect to the web of love.

The Lovetuner and the Universal Field of Love and Unity

All is one and one is all.

We are not separated; we are here all connected. All that is is connected with each other.

We are one with everything.

The creation is revealed as the divine light in our hearts.

We are connected to everything through the universal field

of unity. Our heart is connected—it is one with all the hearts on our planet. In this, the All-One consciousness, we never feel alone because we are protected and sheltered in the All-One. It is our true home as a multidimensional soul.

By being connected to the unity field, we can recognize and thereby express our full creative potential. The vibration of love in our hearts connects us with our true selves. We are here to live unconditional love. We are this unconditional love.

Unconditional love is a divine essence that flows through all beings. It enables us to recognize who we are, where we are coming from, and where we are going.

Living our lives in the unconditional love of life means acknowledging the divine spark within us and discovering our true selves.

The justification of our existence unfolds, and our life acquires meaning. We see the unseen, discover the hidden, and open up our multidimensional consciousness as a soul. The invisible becomes proof through our own experience.

Living our lives in the field of unity means drawing from the basic divine trust. We move from seeker to finder, to the creator of our own life. We put our service into the service of humanity.

We are valuable members of a global community. We bring the best, most superior, and most divine into our lives and thereby serve the good of the community. We set a creative root cause. The effect of this commitment is shown in a life of unconditional love, abundance, joy, freedom, happiness, health, and multidimensional connectedness.

Filled with meaning as part of the wonder of nature. We awaken and live in the unity of being. Connected with above and below. Merging with creation.

The 528 Hz frequency is the frequency of unconditional divine love, and miracles. Through this frequency, the Lovetuner connects each of our trillions of cells within us with the vibration of this field of almighty, eternally knowing, and infinite being. The divine light unfolds within us, and we shine the light into everything around us.

The more we move into the field of unconditional love and unity, the more secure and supported we feel, suspended in the infiniteness of being. We no longer see ourselves as victims but as creators of our own lives and realize that we have never been separated from God.

Love was and will always be there. It is and remains the fundamental component of every single one of our cells in the microcosm as well as in the macrocosm, our universe, and the entire creation for all of us.

When you get to this point in your life, then you can start again to rebuild whatever was not authentic. It doesn't mean the process is slow; it's very fast indeed. You tune in right away, it captures you right away, and it feels good right away.

The only thing you need to do is to keep on tuning to maintain a level of high frequency to be able to receive everything that vibrates on the same high level. Being openhearted allows you to send out and accept only good vibes. Because everything follows the law of nature or the cosmic law. It is impossible to align with low frequencies or negative thoughts when in this state of mind and consciousness.

The best things are always simple. It is a simple concept. Albert Einstein said, "Make it simple but do not make it simpler." This is precisely where we are with this tool, and this is why it literally does not matter what I am telling you.

I mean I am just here to share my experience with you and let you know what the Lovetuner can do; it is really up to you to experience the journey yourself.

You don't have to go anywhere; you don't have to get familiar with complex procedures or time-consuming practices. All you need to do is tune into the 528 Hz frequency and let the Lovetuner open your heart.

When we understand that positive frequencies or high vibrating messages are what we want to align with, it becomes apparent what we have to do: we need to avoid low frequencies. Yet, living unaware in our society makes it nearly impossible to avoid tapping into a low-frequency field.

Our daily lives are usually energy-draining. The simple concept of the Lovetuner makes it easy for everyone to raise one's frequency, instantly attract positive vibes, and become aware of low-swinging energies as they are not in resonance anymore.

As soon as you start using your Lovetuner regularly and make tuning your daily mindfulness practice, positive change will start within you. To change your life and invite positive frequencies you willingly need to let go of low-frequency habits and attachments.

From a bird's-eye perspective, looking down on an airport terminal where all gates are busy, there is no available space for new planes to land. Gates need to be cleared for new passengers to arrive. The same goes for bringing new positive energies into your life. So, before you invite high frequencies, you must let go of all negative vibrations.Don't focus on the outside because you can't control what's happening outside of you. Instead challenge yourself to control how you respond to what's happening. Therein lies your power. After working intensively with frequencies, vibrations, and the Lovetuner, we realize that the power is in the silence. It is why it is essential to remain silent for at least 30 seconds after you finish your lovetuning cycle. The psychological benefits of experiencing silence mean a more purposeful living.

Silence increases self-awareness and self-compassion and improves decision-making as you gain mental clarity. Use this power to become more mindful and self-compassionate.

As the Chinese philosopher Lao Tse said: "Silence is a source of great strength."

Understanding that there is real power in silence, we can learn from this when it comes to how to conduct our conversations and negotiations. The meaning of the power of silence does not lie in exclusion but in inclusion, not in cutting yourself off from people around you but in finding a deeper level of communication. This deeper level of communication enables you to connect to your higher self and your intuition at any time.

Being connected to yourself and your intuition is the basis for successful and productive communication with the outside world. You can achieve this by practicing your daily breathing exercise with your Lovetuner.

Lovetuning will get you to the point of fully experiencing the power of silence and also benefit from the physiological effects, as silence helps to lower high blood pressure, boost your immune system, and regulate brain chemistry by growing new cells.

To fully experience this state of mind, one usually has to commit to a time-consuming daily mindfulness practice. The Lovetuner does all this for you instantly. It gives you an authentic self-empowered experience and frees you from an externally motivated experience of the power of silence. You can achieve all this by yourself. Be your own guru.

Slowly you need to make conscious decisions. You cannot tune into a higher frequency, and on the other hand still keep on drinking, taking drugs, and interacting with people who are negative for you. You cannot spend your time with people that you know you have nothing in common with, only doing so because you have known them for such a long time and being around them has become a habit and has nothing to do with a deep-rooted friendship or connection.

No frequency, no person, and not even the Lovetuner can help you if you are unwilling to change from within. Whatever you do to avoid looking at yourself, whether that is seeing a therapist to talk about how shitty your life is, how bad your parents have been, or how great your parents have been, and what or whomever you are trying to blame for your unhappiness, at the end of the day all this is just a detour and a delay from finding your true self.

Whatever bothers you in your life is irrelevant. If you want to talk about it, you can do this, but nothing will change until you understand that you first have to adjust and raise your frequency. I am not saying don't go to a therapist if something burdensome is happening to you and you need a Band-Aid. Lack of self-empowerment often brings you into the position of not being able to heal yourself.

Seeking an easy way out by giving the responsibility for your life into the hands of others or using sacred medicine without truly respecting those God-given remedies that Mother Earth provides us with is not sustainable. You have to take responsibility for your own life. There is nothing out there that can give you the entire truth.

God only knows the entire truth. When we get closer to the truth, we often go back to the old familiar, and change is simply not happening. We tend to stay in the better-known sorrow than strive for unknown bliss.

The more you trust the world of frequency and vibration, the more you will see that sometimes the person listening to your story is not even in a frequency where they would be able to help you.

Therapy is a tool and a release for many people, but without doing the real work by going within yourself, reflecting on your actions, and driving change from yourself, then you will not be sustainable work in the long run. A therapist cannot be the facilitator of your healing, only you can truly heal yourself. If you do not recognize that change can only occur from within, then you are refusing to take accountability for your role in this life experience and you are not accepting that your actions have a greater impact on this world.

Unless this person whom you are turning to help for has a key to access your heart, is in the light, and has the real power of healing, there is nothing they can do to aid your healing process. Most people are looking for help from outside for their entire life. At one point, they just give up. I have witnessed this happen to people in my life.

At one point in my marriage, I went to therapy, and of course, you can agree on certain things; you can talk about stuff and follow behavioral rules. As it is not experienced on a vibrational, cellular, and emotional level, it will fade away sooner or later.

If you cannot raise your frequency, you will tap into negative frequencies again because they feel familiar, and you will continue to live in dissonance.

You will tap in with your ego and mind, and you will be trapped again. So you go back to therapy, you talk about the shit that happened to you, and you carry on.

It happens when you are not in tune, do not trust yourself, and do not trust the cosmic law of vibration. It spins on and on and on and on. It creates this field of inner conflict where many are trapped in with individuals, families, and most of our society.

Therefore, things escalate all the time because there is never a common ground of vibrational and emotional understanding that gives you the feeling of security. It is like you are building your house on sand.

Not being aware of your frequency, and trying hard to keep your mind busy and entertained is exactly what will not serve you to achieve your goals and live a happy life.

It will not help anybody around you because first, you need to understand to stop talking. Go beyond the blah blah blah. Try to find your core vibration and start raising it constantly. There are tons of mindfulness exercises out there.

Using the Lovetuner, you will first feel your vibration rising. Although being a happy and positive person by nature, the Lovetuner helped me to rebalance all the aspects of my life where I felt trapped in a low-frequency field.

As I said earlier, we are creatures of habit. We frequently remain trapped in the known suffering, painful, and unhealthy relationships due to our affection for our children or societal pressures. The power of the Lovetuner connects you to a divine frequency and makes you aware of what is in harmony or what is in dissonance with yourself.

I figured that it is necessary to frequently check the vibes in any relationship you get into because no matter how many layers you put on top of negative vibes, the truth will come out sooner or later. No material things, lifestyles, or looks will cover this up. Trying to cover the truth with superficial things is unhealthy and unfulfilling.

The Lovetuner and the 528 Hz frequency will not put together what is not in frequency with each other. What I learned from many relationships is that the Lovetuner, in the beginning, helps to raise your harmony and gives you profound happiness.

However, ultimately it will show you precisely what is in resonance with you, what strengthens your relationship, or what you can do to improve or show you very clearly that it is time to leave.

Even if this concept feels abstract to you, if you don't raise your vibration, you cannot expect high-vibrational beings and experiences to come into your life.

CHAPTER V

DECADES

Looking back on my journey at this point in life, reflecting on how I got here and fully understanding what it means to be in flow, I realize that no matter if it is the most beautiful experience or the worst, you cannot hold on to it.

See life as a river, emerging from the spring, constantly moving, and transforming, and finally finding its way into the sea. You don't want to hold on to the banks, and you don't want to drown; you want to be a good swimmer who can enjoy the flow. In ancient Egypt, the Ankh was the symbol of life, and it is referred to as the Key of Life or the Key of the Nile. It is the representative of eternal life.

The bad experiences will transform as much as the good ones. We can never hold on to anything. Living in the here and now means accepting the constant flow. When you do not embrace the present moment you are missing out on the magic of life.

Intellect destroys the magic. We need to examine the biases and preconditions that have been ingrained into us through our upbringing and socialization. This makes up your intellect, and it hinders the magic of the here and now. When we live a life led by our intellect, we are not staying in the present moment. Instead, we are looking to the past and future for answers, instead of embracing the current moment. The here and now is connected to our breath, our heart, and the divine. If we access these three points, then we move from the head into the heart. When you live in the here and now, you are in the heart coherence, not the mind coherence, so you have a higher level of awareness. In the present, you realize that the answers to your questions already exist, and you have access to them. Currently, in our society, the majority of us are not in our heart coherence. Individually, you can always access this, but if we were to collectively move into our heart coherence we would probably be on a different level of communication. It easily overrides the belief systems we have been conditioned in, ridding us of our biases which create disunity in our society.

When we understand that in every second of our lives we are the creator of every thought, we can change anything for the better or the worse. After recognizing this, you can only do one thing, raise your frequency to have higher-vibrational experiences as you enjoy the flow of life.

Many believe that the will to live a spiritual life makes you a better person. The longing to live a spiritual life does not always make you a better person. There is no one-sided experience. If you have not made all your experiences—the good ones and the bad ones—you are not even in the position to decide to become a better person.

Avoiding dealing with the negatives in your life by trying to smile them away is not spiritual at all. It is a lack of authenticity. Genuine and authentic spirituality means you are willing to deal with your inner shadows. You must dig deep, discover them, and deal with them. You can't become a better person and lift your consciousness until you accept to do your shadow work. What makes a strong person is the willingness to overcome their inner shadows and transform them into authentic light. A weak person instead will hold on to their superficial creation of spirituality, avoiding looking deeper.

Let us look at the old Cherokee tale of the two wolves, portraying the good and evil that live in all of us. The tale goes:

One evening, an elderly Cherokee brave told his grandson about a battle that goes on inside people.

He said, "My son, the battle is between two 'wolves' inside us all. One is evil. It is anger, envy, jealousy, sorrow, regret, greed, arrogance, self-pity, guilt, resentment, inferiority, deceit, falseness, pride, superiority, and ego. The other is good. It is joy, peace, love, hope, serenity, humility, kindness, benevolence, empathy, generosity, truth, compassion, and faith."

The grandson thought about it for a minute and then asked his grandfather, "Which wolf wins?"

The old Cherokee simply replied, "The one that you feed."

THERE IS A BATTLE OF TWO WOLVES INSIDE US ALL.

ONE IS EVIL. IT IS ANGER, JEALOUSY, GREED, RESENTMENT, DECEIT, INFERIORITY, AND EGO.

THE OTHER IS GOOD. IT IS JOY, PEACE, LOVE, HOPE, HUMILITY, KIND-NESS, EMPATHY, AND TRUTH.

THE WOLF THAT WINS? THE ONE YOU FEED.

If we are unconscious of our thoughts, we are at the mercy of feeding the evil wolf. Our unconscious thoughts are the unresolved or repressed parts of our psyche. We must acknowledge both the good and the bad in us. It is not about being 100 percent good. If you are 51 percent good, you are already a good person. You need to make a conscious decision about what type of person you want to be. There is no light without a shadow.

It is wishful thinking to be in resonance with yourself and create harmony with the world around you by avoiding looking into the core of things. There is no shortcut to enlightenment. Life is, as we all know, give and take. So when we talk about what is on the inside and outside, everything is reflected and is one experience.

Having been told that being spiritual is being kind, compassionate, and conscious is only one side of the story. The other side of the story is that even the most spiritually aligned among us can still embody some of the worst parts of humanity.

If we understand how this wheel is spinning, we need to look deep into our lives and see and ask ourselves: Have I experienced all feelings? Have I done everything? Have I even entirely been there? Did I understand the entire spectrum? Getting a yes here means you are ready for the journey into the light.

Being true to yourself is the essence. The worst thing you can do is lie. Because you are not lying to someone else, you are lying to yourself. It interferes with the structure of reality itself and damages all possibilities of reaching a higher frequency.

If you are manipulating and lying, you can be very powerful for the short-term, but you create a field of negativity and low frequency and get in resonance with low energies. So, in the long run, you will end up in a terrible crisis.

For the people who still believe in a political instead of a spiritual solution: How can a politician who has been a politician all his life run a country? He simply can't. He is a politician. They can only promote their beliefs.

We cannot rely on a political solution. We need a spiritual revolution. The goal of a spiritual revolution is to raise everyone's consciousness. It is not about having a leader to spring forth a revolution because when people have the power they want to maintain that power, and they can only do so if others are kept on a level below them. In a spiritual revolution, the goal is to elevate everyone to the same level and enter a new stage of consciousness, one beyond a hierarchy. You cannot overcome old patterns by staying in the same consciousness. When we collectively move into a new consciousness it allows for new things to be created. You cannot achieve consciousness and awareness if you are not aware that where there is light, there is also darkness at the same time. Until you acknowledge this duality within us you won't understand that this duality is exactly what we are meant to overcome.

As I said before, the Native Americans knew that there were two wolves in every human being.

One is the mean, the dangerous, the frightened, and then there is the protective, the mild, and the calm. This is not a daily decision but a lifelong one you must make. It's up to you alone to make the right decision. Only you decide which wolf you want to nurture within you.

Looking at the different decades of my journey, in my twenties, all that mattered was the experience and the pleasure of living, not compromising. I started my first business very early when I was still studying architecture at the university, and I tried everything to be free and do what I wanted literally. At that time my motivation was to live wild and free.

From left to right moving down, Sigmar in: Austria 1995, Hungary 1989, Venezuela 1990, Malibu 1994, Marbella 1992, Ibiza 1988

The twenties are known as the decade of trial and error. It is about pushing your boundaries.

For me there was no life in the comfort, I craved extreme. Everything within the boundaries of normal life was boring for me. Very early in life, I was capable of creating my lifestyle. I wanted to be in a position where I never had to work for anybody but for myself. Even as an architecture student, when I was working in an architecture firm, somehow, I always got in a position where I either got a project on my own or was leading a group.

I needed the space to create something and do things for myself. Freedom with what I was doing was key long before I even consciously recognized it.

In retrospect, it was clear that I need this freedom and what I am here for is to create and work independently.

The thirties are the decade of building, it is about establishing yourself, whether that is with a family or career. For me, this decade started still as wild as the twenties ended.

Sigmar, Spain 1998

As the decade progressed, it became the time when I got married and started a family. After that, things started to settle, but I wasn't where I wanted to be. Back then, I was building several companies, and I tried to do many things at the same time. I traveled a lot, but I was not in the right place yet to do what I wanted to do.

All these places, like Austria, or working in Milan and Paris a lot, and then flying to the United States regularly, especially to New York City, were only intermediate stations on my way to true destiny.

Sigmar, NYC, New York 2000

Deep inside, I knew I was not in the right place. Routines and being married to the wrong partner made me feel strangled. I no longer felt that I was able to live wild and free. This was a transitional time for me. I was no longer living just for myself, I had a family that I cared for and now had a responsibility to other people. My life became boring, occupied by trivial conversations and confrontations. It felt to me purposeless. I felt that the life I lived in my twenties was no longer appropriate, yet this new stage felt shallow. I felt I needed to be apologetic for the things in my life that people found extreme, such as kitesurfing. In this next stage of life, I believed I needed to abandon my desire to live wild and free. I felt misplaced in this normal life, and it made me very sad. When I was not busy and trying to build or get stuff done, I was happy to have my kids. The birth of my second child kind of made me forget a little bit that I was not in the place where I wanted to be.

By the end of my thirties, I finally moved overseas with my family. Not to New York City as planned, but to Los Angeles, California. We started to live at the ocean in Malibu, and I had my showroom and manufactory in Santa Monica. It was the time of my life—it was life in Hollywood. My products sold well, and I had a lot of clients from the entertainment industry, many celebrities, and many parties.

I was happy to see my business grow, but at the same time, it had been challenging and a little scary to see—when we talk about fakeness, what LA is about, and what Hollywood stands for.

Sigmar in his Beryll showroom, Santa Monica, California 2007

Yet even at this time, surrounded by superficiality, I was still able to find friends that were also on a spiritual path. I felt a growing urge or curiosity for spirituality that was getting stronger. I started meditating and so on, and I mean I always did extreme sports like kitesurfing; that was something that I was very aware of, even though I didn't consciously sit down and plan a meditation or long-distance swim or extreme sport where you're really in the moment. I started competitively swimming as a kid, and even back then I noticed the meditative state of mind swimming put me in. An exercise like swimming is a meditative practice that involves profound breathwork.

Sigmar kitesurfing, Malibu, California 2014, and Maui, Hawaii 2022

You feel the tremendous power of nature. When you are in the Pacific Ocean; you can feel its power and it reminds you of the connection between us and nature. Those things bring you into the here and now, and that's what it's all about.

The forties are the time for settling down and expanding upon what you built in your thirties. At that time, I built several fashion businesses and expanded my brand. I also began to photograph and paint again and did various exhibitions, continuing my success built in Europe with many nominations and design awards. My work and these awards helped me to become an American citizen with the "alien of extraordinary ability" visa.

One of Sigmar's last paintings in an art series he did in 2012 and 2013 before starting the Lovetuner mission. This painting is called "The Ray of Light." It demonstrates humanity coming out of darkness and into the light.

Spiritually, creativity has long served as a guiding force in my existence, yet it is authenticity that truly bestows rewards, attainable by all through the journey within one's soul.

Meditation, spirituality, and starting Lovetuner helped me to reshape my life. Within a few years, I withdrew more and more from superficial characters.

Even though I was never addicted to anything like alcohol or drugs, it seemed natural to stop drinking. I was aware of the blockade alcohol creates from living to your highest potential and being able to fully embrace the present moment.

Alcohol, with its numbing effects and tendency to lead to addiction, can act as a significant impediment to spiritual growth. Its intoxicating influence can keep individuals trapped in a depressive state, hindering their ability to find clarity, purpose, and inner peace on their spiritual path.

My marriage was not one painted with vibrant hues, the currents of life guided me to flip the page and embark on a new journey. Dwelling in negativity appeared to squander the energy within me. Following my decision to file for divorce, the children chose to remain by my side, and I was granted custody.

My children were the only things that strengthened me and let me play my role as a protector and a father. I felt an instant bond with my children from the moment they were born, but this bond intensified as they became older and I was able to take on a mentorship role.

We started swimming, skiing, surfing and later dirt biking and kitesurfing; it was this bond that made this kind of family life worth having.

After I had, let's call it financial success, and I had established myself and settled in, I realized that no matter what I was going to do in the future, I had a mission to accomplish. At first, I wasn't even sure, and I was experiencing different things, but the urge got stronger, and eventually, it all fell into place.

I have learned that having a family and kids is a wonderful experience in life, but it cannot be your life's purpose. It's meaningful to create life, but no one else's life can be your purpose.

Now I realize that living wild and free does not need to be living extreme, it can be a nice, chill day that is more about your outlook on life. You are not just a numb person going through the motions of life. To be wild and free also means to

Sigmar and his kids, Luis and Adina, Malibu, California 2011

make every moment an active choice in embracing life, not wasting an experience. You can do anything you want anytime in your life.

The 528 Hz frequency experience was indeed the missing link I had been looking for on this journey. Before I knew it, I found myself in the middle of what we know today as the Lovetuner mission. The only thing we had was a belief, a certain feeling, and knowledge. It was more than just faith; I knew exactly what this device was and what needed to be done, even if I did not have a blueprint in hand on how to do it.

The only thing I knew was that I had my way, and if that's what I felt in my heart, then it was definitely going to happen. Of course, some things could have happened faster, some things sooner than we thought, but overall, everything happened at the right time. The universe always delivers.

Now, in my fifties—the decade of knowledge—it's just that, it's the actual dissemination of knowledge. That's precisely where I am now in my life. After all the years of building this company and going my own way, I'm here now to share my knowledge, and I hope this is a life or journey that we all experience at some point. It is the journey from the head to the heart.

You have your wild twenties, you get married in your thirties, you get children, in your forties you settle in, you make money, and then come the fifties, and a lot of people experience a reality check. It is a time that reflection is necessary, and if you are unwilling to examine yourself, then it can be a point where instead of continuing on a higher, spiritual path, you are left with thousands of questions.

What now? Do you want to watch yourself just get older, holding on to the past and worrying about the future? We all know that living in the past causes depression and worrying about the future creates anxiety.

There is no holding on to the past. I look back only when I find pictures; I think it's funny when I talk to an old friend, we talk about old stories—which is all super fun—but I am not living there anymore, that is over, and there are no strings attached where I could say, I missed something or there is something that I did back then that I still want to continue to do. This is exactly what makes it worth getting older because this is the decade of knowledge, and this is where you should strive to be.

What happens so often is that people do the exact opposite; they stay in the past as long as they can, then they are in the here and now and they are not happy because it feels shallow and empty. So, you only have depression when thinking about the past and how life was always better back in the past. Then they look into the future with not even having lived consciously in the here and now.

What do you get out of the future? When you live in the future you get anxiety. The future is not the place where you should be, it is going to come anyway, and there is nothing you can do about it. What you can do is at any time and any second of the here and now you can make a decision, a conscious decision about how your life should be.

The only life worth living is in the here and now. This is true spirituality knowing, doing the right thing and the good thing for the higher and better of yourself, your family, and mankind.

Lovetuner Necklace

CHAPTER VI

528HZ AND SOLFEGGIO FREQUENCIES

My first experience with the 528 Hz frequency was in a guided sound meditation. Although this deep and powerful meditation reminded me of creation—as it is the frequency of the creation, back then I did not experience it on a deeper cellular level because anything you do on a passive level is temporary. I got only a glimpse of this powerful frequency.

The most significant difference between listening to the 528 Hz frequency and tuning into the 528 Hz frequency with the Lovetuner is your active experience while using the Lovetuner.

This active experience settles on a cellular level and will stay in your energetic system, such as chakras, subtle bodies, and most importantly, in your subconscious mind.

The 528 Hz frequency connects you to the creation and awakens your awareness of being a part of the creation. Furthermore, you will understand the real meaning of being the creator of your own life. It is the reason why the 528 Hz frequency has been the "C" note on the musical scale for hundreds of years, as music is harmonious.

The adjustment of our musical scale, bringing in the "A" to from 444 Hz to 440 Hz resulted in the disappearance of the 528 Hz healing frequency.

Musicians, such as John Lennon, who composed the most famous love and peace song, Imagine, in 528 Hz, have not had the power to readjust our musical scale into divine harmony. Hopefully, more and more young musicians will join this 528 Hz revolution to connect hearts and create unity with the power of music.

After getting used to the 528 Hz frequency and tuning for a while, you will reach a higher state of awareness. Tuning into a deeper level of meditation with the Lovetuner enables you to look behind the matrix and enter the fields of creation; you will see the unseen and fully understand the entire journey of mankind, coming from above as a star seed, bringing down the universal love to this planet. You will understand the terms of time and space and unity.

The Lovetuner and the 528 Hz Frequency

Let us have a closer look at frequencies and what they are. Our entire universe is comprised of light, sound, frequency, and vibration. A frequency is always indicated in hertz (Hz), named after the physicist Heinrich Rudolf Hertz, and describes how many vibrations per second trigger a sound. Brain wave frequencies are also referred to in hertz as vibration units. The right frequency is the primary component of healing.

The connections between music, the cosmos, and nature have been known since ancient times.

In 1978 Hans Cousto, a Swiss mathematician and musicologist, compared the frequencies in planetary orbits, in architectural works, in old and modern measuring systems, in the human body, in music, and medicine, and discovered their connections.

What are Solfeggio Frequencies?

Solfeggio frequencies are vibrations and sound frequencies that create a balancing effect on our physical and mental state. The precise 528 Hz frequency can also positively influence and repair our DNA.

Solfeggio frequencies have a healing and health-promoting effect on our body, mind, and soul through our cells and organs' resonance with these frequencies. The vibrations are transferred to our entire organism and can unfold their positive effect. They activate and strengthen our natural self-healing powers. Solfeggio frequencies were already known in ancient times and were used, for example, for Gregorian chants to treat physical and mental ailments.

The original solfeggio frequencies are 396 Hz, 417 Hz, 528 Hz, 639 Hz, 741 Hz, and 852 Hz.

The additional three solfeggio frequencies are 174 Hz, 285 Hz, and 963 Hz.

In music, the 528 Hz frequency refers to the note "Mi" on the scale and is traced back to the expression Mira gestorum (in Latin this means miracle).

Solfeggio frequencies are based on mathematical perfection and can be reduced to the cross-sectional sums of three, six, and nine according to the Pythagorean method of reducing large numbers.

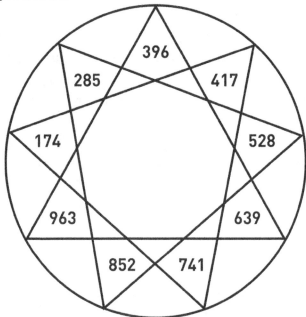

These numbers represent a vector (a vector describes a movement or a displacement in space) of the third and fourth dimensions, the so-called flow field. This field is higher-dimensional energy.

The ancient Greek philosopher Pythagoras taught the perception of the invisible and was one of the first to decipher the mathematics of these sounds.

He was the founder of the mathematical analysis of music and used music as therapy.

The renowned scientist Nikola Tesla points out the importance of these three numbers as the primary indicators of the divine and creative forces. He understood the fundamental law of nature, the universal language of mathematics. A science that has been discovered, not invented, by man. Tesla was aware of the numerical patterns that exist in the universe. They are repeated in star constellations, in the development of embryonic cells, etc.

"If you only knew the magnificence of the 3, 6, and 9, then you would have the key to the universe."

—Nikola Tesla

The Ancient Solfeggio Frequencies
528 Hz—The Magical Frequency

The 528 Hz frequency resonates in the vibration of divine love. It is the frequency of miracles, cell renewal, transformation, divine signs, DNA repair, universal healing, and healing for body, mind, and soul.

Breath and heartbeat are coming into harmony. The frequency of universal love awakens our divine consciousness, and we recognize our true, divine, and creative potential, so to speak. Moreover, we are reminded of our birthright of love, freedom, happiness, and health.

Additionally, the frequency of divine love enhances our creativity, imagination, and intuition.

Through the support of self-healing powers, we obtain more life energy and achieve inner peace and harmony. As a result, we are more empathic and reach the divine states of compassion and unconditional love.

The Physical and Biological Significance of the 528 Hz Frequency

We often talk about the benefits of the ancient solfeggio frequencies and their spiritual and psychological effects. Above all, the 528 Hz frequency has extraordinary physical and biological importance.

The number 528 is found in the geometry of our DNA's spiral shape, which is called a double helix.

The medical pioneer Dr. Royal Raymond Rife, who researched at the beginning of the 20th century, used many frequencies in his practice of radionics, also called electromagnetic therapy.

However, he specifically referred to 528 because of its ability to repair DNA. Dr. Rife used this frequency among hundreds of others for use with his Rife machine, "Radionics." He referred to 528 as "DNA repair."

Molecular genetic investigations have shown that this frequency can be used to repair defective DNA strands or to restore human DNA to its original state. Scientific studies further show that it increases the UV light absorption in DNA and can cure DNA by removing impurities that cause disease.

In 2017 a study by the Biochemical Institute of the University of Tehran was published in the Journal of Addiction and Therapies. The study's objective: to prove that the consumption of alcohol is a major problem in human society due to its harmful effects on various tissues, including the nervous system.

Today, the use of non-pharmacological and noninvasive agents is quite common. Sound waves, which are classified as noninvasive means for stimulating auditory cells, also affect non- auditory cells. Since the frequency of 528 Hz is related to the musical note "Mi," effects such as an increase in the ability to repair DNA are observed.

Cells treated with a combination of ethanol and 528 Hz tones at 80 dB exhibited a marked reduction in reductive oxygen species (ROS), also known as oxygen radicals, and thus a reduction in cell death due to severe alcoholism.

The current results indicate that in the ethanol extract (IC50), the frequency of 528 Hz increased the viability of the cells by about 20 percent and reduced the level of oxygen radical production by up to 100 percent.

The use of these sound frequencies can be beneficial in reducing the toxic effects of alcohol on brain cells.

This could not only prove to be an effective means of treating damage to the central vascular system in people with alcoholism, or even in babies born to alcoholic mothers, but also be an indicator of the positive effects of 528 Hz on cellular health in general.

The positive effects of DNA repair through the 528 Hz frequency are increased life energy, mental clarity, conscious perception, awakened activated creativity, and ecstatic states like deep inner peace and joy.

In this respect, Dr. James Gimzewski of UCLA discovered that individual cells produce sounds and that different cells have different sound signatures or vibrations.

Although this form of investigation, known as sonocytology, is a comparatively new science, the theoretical implications are tremendous. As an example, Dr. Gimzewski is hoping to destroy harmful cells by using their natural frequencies without damaging the surrounding cells.

The following gives an insight into the synergy of the 528 Hz frequency and nature:The 528 Hz frequency is the most important of the historical solfeggio frequencies. It has a deep connection to nature and is found in grass/chlorophyll, oxygen, rainbows, sunlight, and the buzzing of bees.

These images from a microscope show a water molecule being brought back to its perfect hexagonal shape as it is tuned to 528hz

The image above shows the Lovetuner crystal. These pictures were taken with a microscope and depict water molecules tuned into the 528 Hz frequency with the Lovetuner. These images prove that the water molecules regress to a perfect hexagon shape.

Water that is clustered in a six-sided or hexagonal shape is of incredible importance for the structure and health of our DNA. The 528 Hz frequency can positively influence water cell clusters and support the elimination of toxins. Bio-resonance test measurements demonstrated up to a 90-percent improvement in vital functions.

This physical reaction during tuning can be felt in the entire body on a cellular level because our body consists of more than 70 percent water, and our blood consists of more than 90 percent water. The alignment of the molecules to the perfect form helps to achieve an immediately noticeable level of relaxation, and dissolves stress and anxiety.

The work of Dr. Lee Lorenzen, who discovered the clustered healing water, demonstrated that the 528 Hz frequency contributes to creating these six-sided water clusters.The universal law of vibration indicates that all matter and molecules constantly move and vibrate.

When we vibrate normal water at the 528 Hz frequency, it begins to vibrate synchronously and creates the crystal-shaped, high-energy water clusters that form the DNA's protective matrix. The biochemist Steve Chemiski points out in his book A Fork In The Road, that the water clusters vibrate at precisely 528 cycles per second.

Although this effect is indirect, it is the most remarkable example of the potential of 528 Hz to heal our DNA. Professor Richard J. Saykally and other geneticists at UC Berkeley have performed experiments proving that reducing the access of a strand of DNA to these energized water clusters impairs its ability to function correctly. Dehydrated DNA is less energetic and not as healthy.

When tuned at the 528 Hz frequency, the perfect water cell clusters are smaller and manage to move better through the membrane of DNA than normal water molecules, allowing them better to remove contaminants from the cells of our body, creating a healthier cellular environment capable of curing or preventing disease.

Following the notorious BP oil spill in the Gulf of Mexico in 2010 that an explosion on the drilling platform known as Deepwater Horizon caused, John and Nancy Hutchinson used 528 Hz and other asolfeggio frequencies to treat the water. After only four hours of exposure, they were able to reduce the amount of oil and grease in an ocean section from seven parts per million to only one part per million.

This incredible achievement was later confirmed by Dr. Robert Naman and the Analytical Chemical Testing Laboratory, Inc.

CHAPTER VII

TUNE IN EVERYTHING IS FREQUENCY AND VIBRATION

We are all here, in this time and this space. We all share the same experience.

We bear witness to the evolution of humanity and consciousness. Together, in unity. Each one of us has our own experiences. Each of us is unique. There are no two identical experiences. They can be beautiful, painful, or intense.

We all share the same dreams and hope to experience love

and peace in our lives.

Now is the time to unite and support each other on our human journey—creating harmony, peace, and coherence through love and the power of a single frequency to bring healing to our lives, bodies, minds, spirits, and planet.

As we all know from personal experience, all we need is love. So, when I started to understand higher consciousness and how I can facilitate this to humanity with the Lovetuner, my main question was: how do we all unify and get there?

The deeper I dropped into the field of frequency and vibration, the clearer my downloads became, and at one point, I received the answers:

We need to remind ourselves of the power of our hearts and the power of love, and through feeling the love that already exists in all of us and connecting us, we create harmony, coherence, love, and compassion.

The Big Bang

Soon after starting Lovetuner, I received many testimonials that differed from my initial idea of the Lovetuner being a powerful mindfulness tool and a shortcut to meditation. Numerous field reports from random people I did not even know have been beyond magical.

One that still touches my heart today was from a yoga teacher giving a lesson in Thailand. During her class, she witnessed a lady who collapsed on the street with her baby in her arms. The yogi ran out to the street, where the young woman was lying on the ground, unconscious, seemingly to be suffering from a heart attack or a stroke. People had been already gathering around the woman and her baby. Out of her intuition, the yogi touched the woman's heart and started tuning. Within a minute, the woman came back to life.

I received many of those testimonials, all the way into reports from people running tantric love seminars. They used the Lovetuner for the first time in their workshops. They experienced a sexually energetic, heartfelt connection that they have not been a part of in over a decade-long engagement in this field.

As I started to work with schools and children, I could not even publish any of those experiences that have been reported to me. It would not have allowed me to work with schools or even get serious recognition in the health and well-being industry. Yet, allowing and accepting this magic into my consciousness made me search and dig deeper into the beginning of sound and frequency, the Big Bang.

EVOLUTION OF THE UNIVERSE

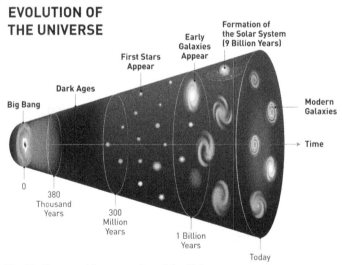

The Big Bang and the expansion of the Universe

The Big Bang was followed by the expansion of the universe into three-dimensional space. The graph with the time axis shows the Big Bang's development to the present over 13.7 billion years.

Everything in the universe is made of tones.

Everything in the universe is sound.

Everything in the universe is vibration.

Therefore, it has a specific vibrational frequency. This also applies to our thoughts, feelings, and emotions. So does love. Love has a specific vibrational frequency of 528 Hz, the love frequency.

What does this mean for our human experience? At no time in human history has there been an attempt to create coherence on this planet through the power of a single frequency. This 528 Hz is audible in the center of our musical scale—the "C" by raising the "A" to 444 Hz, visible in the middle of our color spectrum, through the wavelength of 528 nm, in the color light green—which can be sensed in the middle of our body, in our heart center.

The frequency 528 Hz is part of the sacred solfeggio tones and is synonymous with wonder, DNA repair, and transformation. This is even reflected in the color 528 nm, green is the color of healing.

This allows us to connect and feel grounded, peaceful, and loving. Imagine putting a candle into a dark room, the room is illuminated, and the darkness disappears.

The same principle applies to the Lovetuner. When you tune and invite love into your body, stress and fear disappear. If we consider that the universe was created out of love and if we take into account that we were also created out of love, it makes sense that the 528 Hz is the frequency that connects us with what we are. We are love. Love is the cause and the result. The way, the solution, the truth.

Nothing is more accurate than the experience of living one vibrational energy—the vibrational frequency of love for life. The principle of resonance states that if one object vibrates simultaneously with a second object, the second object is automatically placed into the same vibrational motion.

Now imagine that you are the second object and the vibration of the Lovetuner brings out the love that naturally exists within you and aligns your vibrational frequency with the frequency of love.

The next logical step for me was to investigate the power of our hearts in more detail. I discovered many scientific research reports that showed when we experience stress and anxiety, our heart rate variability becomes erratic and chaotic.

When we experience love and compassion, our heart rate variability is in harmony.

Our hearts are electromagnetic field generators indeed. The electromagnetic field of the heart is 5,000 times stronger than our mind. It affects not only our body but also the heart field; it can also be measured up to 7.5 meters (24 feet) in the energy field surrounding us.

The heart is also classified as a hormonal gland that secretes hormones and neurotransmitters which profoundly affect our brain and bodily functions. For example, oxytocin is known as the binding or love hormone because it brings things together with feelings of compassion, harmony, love, and peace. Our mind receives much of its information from the heart.

So, the heart is in a state of unity, while the mind is in a state of duality, like the right and left sides of the brain.

Therefore, we should listen to our hearts and acknowledge them as the true gateway to peace.

My musical tastes range from classical music to rock, and to electronic music, which I presented in nightclubs, events, and big dance parties in the 90s. From smaller nightclubs to large dance parties and raves, I experienced how the desire of many people at that time was to dance, be in trance, have a good time, and feel connected.

The 90s was a decade of trance music, especially in Europe, the birthplace of this music. Trance music incorporates mind-altering sounds, which creates an elevated atmosphere and gives a euphoric feeling to listeners. Even though it was not a spiritual way of connecting back then, the power of the music, the beat, and the groove made people come together.

Educating and bringing awareness to musicians and DJs became a big part of the Lovetuner movement, as every revolution has its music. The in-tune music from the divine source we are creating is the music of the spiritual revolution.

In the following, I would like to share a fascinating study that investigated the stress-reducing effect of music with the frequency of 528 Hz on the endocrine and autonomic nervous systems, which has recently become known as "healing" music.

Generally speaking, this particular type of music, which uses a 528 Hz scale, is called solfeggio frequency music. Various effects have been attributed to the solfeggio frequency, but no scientific basis has been found for it until now. This study provides new evidence for its use in music therapy.

Typically, the reference tone of tuning is 440 Hz, the international standard frequency (we refer to this as 440 Hz music). In this scale, there is no 528 Hz note.

However, setting the reference tone to 444 Hz means that 528 Hz is included in the scale.

Therefore, music that is tuned and composed in this manner is called 528 Hz music.

We know that listening to music reduces stress. Research has examined many aspects of this phenomenon, and it is widely recognized that several constituent elements of music are involved in this stress-reducing effect. Previous studies that examined emotional arousal in response to listening to music suggest that music causes different emotions depending on its characteristics such as melody, rhythm, and dynamics.

However, so far, only some studies have investigated how the differences in the frequency of music affect the human body. The results suggest that the influence of music on the autonomic nervous and endocrine systems varies depending on the frequency of the music. The music at 528 Hz has a particularly powerful stress-reducing effect, even after only five minutes of exposure.

In the 528 Hz state, the mean cortisol values (stress values) decreased significantly; chromogranin A declined gradually—among other things, a low chromogranin A value has positive effects on the function of the pancreas (pancreas), the parathyroid glands, as well as on the immune and the cardiovascular system. Oxytocin—also called the body's bonding hormone—was significantly increased after exposure to music. A high level of oxytocin is responsible for reducing anxiety and stress; it reduces aggression, allows us to build trust in other people, and makes us empathic.

Tension, anxiety, and mood swings were significantly reduced after exposure to 528 Hz music, while there was no significant difference after 440 Hz music.

In summary, this study concluded that the participants experienced an objective and subjective stress reduction after listening to music at 528 Hz, whereas this effect could not be confirmed for music at 440 Hz.

Music with different frequencies was found to have different effects on the endocrine system, especially oxytocin, and cortisol. In addition, the results show that music at 528 Hz reduces stress, even if the participants listen to the music only for a short period.

Thanks to the participants for their voluntary cooperation and to the Institute of Man and Science Inc. for analyzing the electrocardiogram data.

Based on this effect, I created the following Lovetuner Tune Up!, a very effective and fun way to connect your Lovetuner to the high vibrations of the music in 528 Hz and dance into higher consciousness.

The Lovetuner and the Tune Up! Dance Experience

The Lovetuner Tune Up! is a meeting of like-minded people who like dancing, practicing yoga, and meditating.

We enjoy a positive, healthy lifestyle and seek to replace late-night clubbing, drugs, and alcohol with our passion for dancing and healthy fun.

The Tune-Up! covers exactly this field and builds a whole new community. It brings us together early in the morning after a relaxing night's sleep and is held in nightclubs with state-of- the-art sound and lighting systems.

Our DJs become trainers and vibration masters to make this a powerful body, mind and spirit experience. The music is based on high beats per minute (bpm), similar to deep house and trance music, which are remixed on a sound carpet of 528 Hz, the so-called Love Frequency, and accompanied by the rhythm of live drums.

The frequency of 528 Hz is the frequency of our hearts, and the drums represent our heartbeats.

This constant beating is a meditative sound that puts us into a trance. Trance and meditation are vehicles that put us in the state of "No Mind." We wear yoga or workout gear as the venue is similar in temperature to a hot yoga class.

Positive affirmations are mixed into the 60-minute Tune Up! dance experience and lead us to our highest self. We sweat, dance, and share a unique experience. Then, we finish the Tune-Up! event with a group session where we tune with the Lovetuner and repeat self- affirming mantras to strengthen the feeling of unity and to help us take those feelings with us as we return to daily life.

General Procedure:

Find a quiet space inside or outdoors in nature where you will not be disturbed.

Please set your cell phones to silent.

Ask the group for their attention and respect and give the same back to them.

Position yourself and the group in a way you can look into each other's eyes. You can conduct this session in a seated or standing position.

Relaxed eye contact creates good vibes and a feeling of safety for you and your counterpart.

Next, give a brief explanation of how to use the Lovetuner. Begin by explaining and demonstrating how to use the Lovetuner.

Remove the Lovetuner from its cover and place the end with the engraved Lovetuner logo between your lips.

Take a deep breath and exhale gently with a suspended breath into the Lovetuner as if it were a flute or recorder, creating an even and gentle tone.

You don't need to use too much force; the volume of the sound is not important.

An even tone and a smooth, consistent sound are key.

Exhale as slowly and as long as possible, keeping the tone smooth and gentle.

For the best results, inhale through your nose and exhale through the Lovetuner flute.

Let your breath circulate through your body as you inhale and produce sound as you exhale.

When you are finished, put your Lovetuner back into the cap.

Now ask the group to pull out the Lovetuner and be ready to use it during the session.

Follow with a relaxing body, mind, and spirit post-Tune Up! Mantras.

Read the mantras aloud in a relaxed, moderate tone, modulating your voice to accommodate the acoustics of the space as you tune in "live" with the Lovetuner, either alone or with the group.

Turn the music on.

When you are finished with the mantras, give yourself and the group a moment to let the good vibes linger before you return to your daily routine. If you have the opportunity and are comfortable with it, you are welcome to ask for feedback and exchange ideas. Thank everyone for the time spent together, and withdraw.

Read each mantra or affirmation out loud, allowing the others to repeat it to you. Then, intuitively select all or a subset of the mantras and use as many repetitions as you feel you need. Most important: feel free and have fun!

- One World.
- One Love.
- One Tone.
- One Journey.
- I am Divine Love.
- I am Divine Light.
- I am Soul.
- I am All That Is.
- I am Grateful.
- I am Pure Love.
- I am Pure Light.
- I am Pure Frequency.
- I am Limitless.
- I am a Vibration.
- I am a Miracle Magnet.
- I am a Vibration of Unconditional Love.
- I am a Vibration of Universal Love.
- I am a Vibration of Higher Love.
- I am Vibrating Unconditional Love.
- I am Vibrating Divine Light.
- I am Vibrating Happiness.
- I am Vibrating Freedom and Abundance.
- I am Vibrating Peace.
- I am Vibrating Light and Love.
- I am the Essence of Divine Love.
- I am a Vessel for Divine Light.

- I am a Strong Creator.
- I am the Creator of My Own Life.
- I am the Creator of My Reality.
- I am Radiating Love for Myself and Love for All That Is.
- I am Radiating Universal Light.
- I am Radiating Positive Energy.
- I am Transmitting Frequency.
- I am Transmitting Gratitude.
- I am Transmitting Divine Love.
- I am Transmitting Divine Light.
- I am Choosing the Frequency of Light.
- I am Choosing the Frequency of Love.
- I am Choosing the Frequency of Happiness.
- I am Choosing the Frequency of Freedom.
- I am Choosing the Frequency of Abundance.
- I am Choosing the Frequency of Peace.
- I am in Perfect Alignment with My Higher Self.
- I am in Perfect Alignment with Unconditional Love.
- I am in Perfect Alignment with Divine Light.I am in Perfect Alignment with My Soul.
- I am in Perfect Alignment with the Source.
- I am Connected to the Universal Light.
- I am Connected to the Source.
- I am Connected to Universal Love.
- I am Connected to All That Is.
- I am Connected to All Beings.
- I am Connected to All Hearts.
- I am the Universal Infinite Stream of Prosperity and Abundance.
- I am Choosing the Frequencies I Transmit.

- I am Choosing to Send Out the Frequency of Unconditional Love, Health, Prosperity, Peace, and Joy.
- I am Aware that Whatever Frequency I am Sending Out is Coming Back to Me.

Pioneers that brought back awareness about the 528 Hz frequency and rediscovered this forgotten knowledge, like Dr. Leonard Horowitz and Dr. Joseph Puleo, published many valuable studies that I would like to refer to.

With the 528 Hz frequency, your life will never be the same again. It was discovered that the frequency of 528 Hz belongs to almost the exact center of the frequency of the entire electromagnetic color spectrum. There is only one number in the entire numerical system in which the electromagnetic color spectrum is the same—the sound system.

This one number is 528, the same in both color and sound— the 528 Hz frequency.

A miraculous key that opened doors that no one had closed and closed doors that no one could open. This 528 will change your life most beneficially! We now have substantial evidence, vast amounts of evidence, that 528 is the key to this.Ultimately what is happening to this planet is that we are in dissonance with another note, another frequency. When we discovered the original musical scale, it turned out that there were not only six, but a total of nine creative core frequencies in the universe. Everything in the universe is made of nine notes. Only nine! And that the first six are the solfeggios and that there are three more that form a perfect circle of sound.

This perfect sound circle looks something like this:

Graphically depicted, the first six notes are 396, 417, 528, 639, 741, 852; the original solfeggio scale.

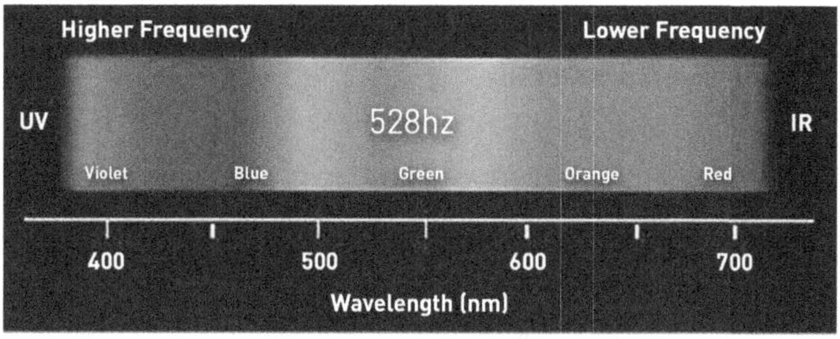
Higher Frequency
Lower Frequency
UV
528hz
IR
Violet
Blue
Green
Orange
Red
400
500
600
700
Wavelength (nm)

528 Hz is the only number in the entire numeric system, whereby the electromagnetic color spectrum is the same as the sound system. It's like the heart of a rainbow. Color = 528 Hz = Sound

In the image above, you can see that 528 is the color green. It is the heart of the rainbow; it is the wonderful tone of the solfeggio scale.

The other note, 741, which is part of nature, is called "the devil's interval" in musicology. If you play 741 with 528, such an annoying and dissonant energy arises; so sick and stressful that you could die if you continue to listen!

This is an interesting concept! In today's world, some people control practically everything economically and geopolitically. Their agenda is to manipulate the population for thousands of years!

They have the secret knowledge, the ancient music, with which the pyramids were constructed based on mathematics. The entire universe is built on these nine tones—they knew about them! In fact, in 1939 they founded the Rockefeller Foundation, which introduced the worldwide standard for tuning.

The Western world set the A440 Hz frequency, which means that when you tune your instrument, you set it so that the "Fis" note is exactly 741!

The A440 is now the default setting. When you choose A439, you are much closer to it; when you choose A441, you are closer to one of the Creator's original sounds. That's exactly how it was manipulated!

To do what exactly?

To turn off 95 percent of your brain, especially the right hemisphere, which serves the divine-human community's heart-mind.

So, you understand what we're talking about here is a metaphor—when you are driving and your radio is tuned to a station, you are listening to music. You love music! If you move further away from the transmitter tower, the music starts to rustle. You lose the broadcast signal with a clear channel, and now there is background noise.

You might be a little annoyed, but you still want to listen to the music, so you listen to it for another 10 km or around six miles. Suddenly it gets so annoying that you are disgusted and turn it off. If you were to keep listening, you would get sick.

That's what we're talking about here, except that you don't even know that you've been listening to that so-called noise all your life. You don't even know what the true resonant frequency is because it has been withheld from you!

In other words, the master composer, the master conductor of the Universal Orchestra, sings love songs at the frequency of 528 and raises everything at the same time!

And we are the only species that is out of tune and accepts noise as a clear channel.

Dr. Masaru Emoto takes the stage and has a musical triangle, which he plays, like in an orchestra. And he tunes it over here, and about 30 feet away, his interpreter is standing with a reproduction of a triangle of equal size tuned to the equal frequency. And he tells his interpreter to put a microphone next to it, and suddenly it starts to vibrate. He hits the microphone over there, and suddenly it starts to vibrate.

How much of your body is made up of water?

When I was at Harvard University taking public health classes, the truth of the matter is it is about 86 percent. Consequently, 85 percent of your well-hydrated body is water.

Today we are told that this number is only 75 percent! You have been dehydrated with the toxins! A total of 93 percent of the function of DNA is light and sound, reception, and transmission. Photon, phonon, reception, transmission for intercellular communication, and cellular up-regulation.

Do you know what cellular up-regulation is?

It signifies precipitation in the now, in every millisecond. In every second you are currently re-manifesting in water of all materials; water is the most energy-conductive! It is a superconductor.

Allow me to tell you about the fundamental vibration, the root of the Mantri origin of the numbers: The most important numbers are three, six, and nine.

And Tesla, who created the Tesla coil, was right once again: Tesla coils are energy amplifiers.

Their DNA is an energy amplifier, a coil that works mainly with three, six, and nine.

For those of you who do not know what I am talking about, have you ever looked at machines or motors? They are magnets wrapped in copper wire. If you wrap copper around the magnet, the energy increases dramatically!

That is exactly what your DNA is. It is an antenna for the Creator. Every single cell in your body has this energy capacity. It contains this divine intelligence.

What does that mean?

It means that the first beings you should communicate with to uplift yourself, receive, and heal are the billions of cells in your own body that have their unique genetic intelligence, sacred to the Creator. This is the very structure of how the universe works, which is fantastic for us. Our understanding of some of the most wonderful information enables us to live in trust. Life according to the law, according to the matrix.

Here is a simple way to analyze this:

You have probably heard of "The way you treat others is how others will treat you," or "As you sow, so shall you reap." That explains it all. Let us assume you are here and releasing negative thoughts and relationships. Negative actions, all energy. The neurology in your brain is quite powerful! 86 percent of you is made up of creation water.

And here is what happens next. It goes out, it goes up, and it goes out again. This is called the "Event Horizon." What you send through the center of the Event Horizon, that is, through the black hole, turns around and returns; it comes back immediately and brings you karma; it brings you divine judgment. It all corresponds to the mathematical matrix, that's for sure. And mathematics do not lie; they are always constant. Nothing is missing, nothing is broken.

There are claims that the 432 Hz frequency is the central solfeggio frequency in nature and the universe. They discredit the 528 Hz vibrating in the heart of the rainbow and the heart chakra (greenish, yellow-green is the color of healing) by promoting 432 Hz as an alternative.

According to common sense, the sacred geometry, electrochemistry, and biophysics of chlorophyll, which appear in a greenish-yellow color, vibrate at the frequency of 528 Hz, while the 432 Hz frequency oscillates in a dark navy-blue color.

The 528 frequency is clearly about love, peace, and freedom, and 432 has been chosen by agents of fear, war, and mental enslavement to defeat the "528 Hz Love Revolution."

CHAPTER VIII

THE GLOBAL LOVE & PEACE MISSION

For me, Lovetuner was and still is a love and peace mission to unify humanity and bring healing into our world. As I was an entrepreneur and designer who launched multiple international brands, the business side, and the strategy for the Lovetuner was solid.

However, I had to learn that whatever was not in resonance with the Lovetuner, and the people I had worked with for many years, that just did not have the proper resonance, would have to fall off the wagon for multiple reasons. Also, people who joined for the wrong reasons could not sustain this clear and powerful frequency as this frequency does not accept anything less than divine intentions.

We got fantastic feedback from people using the Lovetuner, and given the nature of my hometown, Malibu, California, celebrities became dedicated Lovetuner users pretty quickly. From a business point of view, it meant a good start, but my intention was not to create a seasonal esoteric gimmick, but a sustainable movement with a higher purpose and a global impact.

At the beginning of the Lovetuner journey, I was confused that many things did not align in the three-D world as I expected.

Over time, I figured you could not treat a divine mission like an everyday business. When I started to accept this and dedicated all my energy to this mission, a significant transformation began, and the frequency took the lead. I knew I had to go deeper and further into this mission to spread the love and start right where the most important impact can be made: the next generation. Our future!

"If every 8 year old in the world is taught meditation, we will eliminate violence from the world within one generation." (Dalai Lama)

Simultaneously with the launch of the Lovetuner, we created the Lovetuner mindfulness class for elementary schools. In addition, we went into public and private schools to introduce the Lovetuner to the kids and their teachers. Within one year, we gathered a lot of positive feedback. Kids and teachers alike reported that bullying was eliminated. Kids became more focused, got better grades, and all over felt better vibes toward each other.

At the end of the school year, kids started to ask to even have more lovetuning classes, and the first kids who graduated in that school year made a colorful book for us with drawings. Every little drawing started with "Because of the Lovetuner …" and stated what improved in their lives and how tuning positively affected their family life.

Here are some actual testimonials from eight-year-olds about their experiences with the Lovetuner:

"Because I have my LOVETUNER, I know what to do when I'm stressed."

"Because I have my LOVETUNER, I know the key of love." (through the 528 Hz frequency of love created by tuning).

"Because I have my LOVETUNER, I now know what to do when I get angry."

"Because I have my LOVETUNER, I can calm down better and faster."

Our research shows that children react extremely positively to the Lovetuner and lovetuning.

The 528 Hz frequency of unconditional love has a strong and very positive effect on the entire atmosphere in schools.

From a spiritual perspective, starting to tune with kids as early as possible makes sense. Even preschool children will benefit from tuning. The souls of our children are still very connected to the higher field of universal love. Lovetuning will help these sensitive souls get grounded and prepare them to connect with our planet.

Growing up, we get used to listening more to our minds than to our hearts. We put logic before feelings, creating layers of density and losing the connection to our souls and intuition. A big awareness started in the past decades recognizing higher vibrational light coming down to our planet. Today's generation and the ones to come are on a different level of vibration than past generations. These children are already starting on a high-vibrational level, whereas prior generations still have much work to do to get there. We must support and nurture our future generations in unfolding their full spiritual potential.

Our society is so used to living a disconnected life. Instead of experiencing nature, and in general life naturally and in a practical way, we got used to getting our experiences online. Being aware of this, we can support our kids by being role models and showing them that real life is there to be experienced by using our nature-given senses instead of replacing them with AI. We are responsible for looking behind the matrix and protecting our children from being sucked into this heartless electronic reproduction of life. No matter how advanced, to a certain degree technology is for humanity—the artificial cyber world has nothing to do with the real point of life and the here and now. Only in the here and now living in its purest form is possible.

The metaverse is the next level of being disconnected from real life. Suppose people in the mindfulness industry, like healers and so-called spiritual guides, supported this matrix. In that case, they are disconnecting and separating humans even more from their natural ability to discover their true feelings.

It takes away the healing magic of nature needed for a supernatural being to have a human experience. It disconnects us from our unique vibration or frequency, which is the essence of who we are.

Humankind is on the verge of a universal spiritual awakening. The golden age is knocking on all our doors. By understanding how complex adults have to work on their ability to get back to their divine core, we are forced to stop wasting time with material distractions and prepare ourselves to strip off all human layers of greed, envy, and competitiveness.

As adults, we have disconnected ourselves from the connection to the higher consciousness that our children and the next generation still have. That which is given to them by nature, we experience again later in life when we realize that we are just not happy. Then, when we reach the next level of escalation and become mentally confused or depressed, only then do we turn back to what is naturally given to us. It is our stage of spiritual awakening.

We begin to observe our patterns and behaviors, and we begin to feel a sense of connectedness, to let go of attachments, and find inner peace find that our natural intuition returns, and we experience synchronicity. We increase our compassion and lose the fear of death, which is as natural in the cycle of life as birth.

The past years of living in a pandemic world have driven us even further apart. Unfortunately, the harmful extent of what was done to our children and younger generations by purposely misguiding parents and children alike has not yet fully unfolded.

With disconnected people, it is easy to outline everything that already separates us, and out of thin air, causalities are created to abuse diversity. Pushing the agenda of under-education and entitlement is bringing our society to the verge of collapse.

Given those circumstances, we are responsible for creating an alternative to this sick system.

Research shows a harmonizing effect of mindfulness and meditation by using the Lovetuner.

Negativity, bullying, anxiety, and violence can be changed positively and sustainably.

Lovetuning generates a high vibration, so joy, lightness, concentration, healthy activity, communication, and the feeling of unity, the we-feeling, are supported and promoted.

With the Lovetuner no previous knowledge is required, unlike with everyday meditation. Three to five minutes of tuning with the Lovetuner achieves the same effect as twenty minutes of meditation. With the Lovetuner, mindfulness becomes a playful experience for children, students, and teachers.

Lovetuning can be easily integrated into the daily school routine and be part of the curriculum.

Using the Lovetuner helps with reducing commotions in class; it makes sense for calming down and decelerating. The Lovetuner supports conflict resolution between students or the prevention of conflicts. It helps to master increasing demands in everyday school life more efficiently and reduces anxiety in exam situations. Tuning supports the students with focus and concentration and creates motivation to process extensive teaching material.It gives them the courage to express their thoughts and feelings positively and beneficially. The feeling creates harmony and brings lightness and joy into the daily school routine. Tuning at school events manifests the feeling of unity and community spirit.

Overall, positive emotions such as love, gratitude, peace, and balance, are actively generated with the Lovetuner and have a harmonious effect on the interaction of students and teachers.

As a result, everyday school life becomes more pleasant and more effortless.

Furthermore, a high-vibrational state also improves communication, an essential factor in teaching. All in all, everyone involved benefits from using the Lovetuner in the school sector because relaxed teachers attract relaxed students in the resonance and vice versa.

High frequencies generate good vibrations, and students and teachers take these positive vibrations home with them. In this way, good vibes are transferred to all areas of life. Both professionally and privately, there is an increase in the quality of life.

Here are specific insights into the benefits of the Lovetuner in the classroom:

The Lovetuner supports the teacher and aids classroom management by:

- Reducing restlessness, thus promoting calm and de-escalating aggression.
- Supporting conflict resolution between students and adults and even mitigating conflict before it becomes of issue.
- Helping students master the increasing demands of everyday school life.
- Reducing fear and test anxiety.

- Promoting student focus and concentration.
- Supporting motivation to create and process extensive teaching material.
- Promoting and aiding in the development of higher-order thinking skills.
- Encouraging students to express thoughts and feelings in a calm, relaxed manner.
- Creating harmony in the classroom with the concept of ".".
- Bringing light and joy into everyday school life.
- Creating joyful breaks during the school day.
- Supporting educators with a way to release stress quickly and effectively in the teacher's lounge.
- Supporting the student body and school events by manifesting school pride, unity, and spirit.

The positive emotions of love, gratitude, peace, and balance can be actively generated through the Lovetuner, creating a harmonious effect on the interaction between students and teachers.

As a result, the school day becomes more pleasant and easier to navigate.

Furthermore, the high vibration created by the Lovetuner also results in better communication, an essential factor in the classroom.

All in all, participants can benefit immensely from using the Lovetuner in schools because relaxed teachers create and influence relaxed students through a calming resonance and vice versa.

High frequencies generate positive vibrations, which students and teachers can take home with them. Thus the good vibes are transferred to all areas of life and into the community, supporting the possibility of an increase in the quality of life for all.

Elementary School Classroom Experiences

The Lovetuner Program has been successfully implemented in various classrooms with elementary school students aged six to 10 years. The program uses movement (e.g., dance and movement meditation) to awaken the emotional self through humor and cheerfulness, thus promoting and strengthening intuition and supporting the development of socio-emotional learning (SEL).

The Lovetuner, when used at the beginning, during, or at the close of the school day, integrates learning support, stress reduction, harmony, and cooperation in the classroom.

1st grade: The teacher called the Lovetuner a "magic whistle" that brings a good mood and delights the heart. At the beginning of each unit, she implemented three tuning breathing cycles while the children put their hands on their hearts to help them focus on the feelings the 528 Hz sound created.

Some children reported that the Lovetuner made them feel calm; others found it energizing and had an impulse to move or jump; others thought it sounded funny. Another student reported, "It was warm." Generally, students felt much more relaxed after the tuning session. The harmonic tone resulted in a desire for movement in some; in the truest sense of the word, the heart began to jump and showed itself in the joy of movement.

2nd grade: This classroom teacher was already a regular user of the Lovetuner before using it with the students. When brought into the classroom, it was clear that the children became much more relaxed, particularly versus children from other classes who had not experienced the Lovetuner.

Feedback from the children: "calm," "a warm feeling," "beautiful"; some felt the urge to talk after tuning, some said they felt "tired," others felt more relaxed and experienced calm, a "warm feeling" and "feeling beautiful."

The experience allowed the children to move into a relaxed but energetic state more easily. The students always wanted to tune in more because they liked it so much. It made them feel good!

3rd grade: This class was challenging, very energized, and sometimes frenetic. One time tuning was accepted, but another time it was resisted. As a result, it was necessary to add additional tuning cycles before and during the session. In addition, some students became emotional as the tuning opened and activated their hearts.

4th grade: The classroom teacher had previously practiced meditation with the children. As a result, the children were very open and accessible to the Lovetuner. The children found it very pleasant and seemed more centered after tuning.

Verbal feedback from the children included the words: "beautiful," "warm," "calm," and "big."

Conclusion: Overall, the students thoroughly enjoyed the Lovetuner and willingly accepted its use in the classroom. In addition, students reported experiencing positive results from tuning and were more relaxed after tuning than before the start of each session.

CHAPTER IX

DEEPER INTO THE JOURNEY

Getting more into tuning, I realized that it became my mission with the Lovetuner to help to make this world a better place. In the beginning, it felt selfish to heal me, until I reached the point where it became clear to me that healing myself means healing the collective.

Deeper into the journey, I recognized that it is all about tuning into yourself, meaning you are becoming constantly aware of vibrations and understanding that you are the creator of your frequency.

When the Lovetuner meditation and breathing exercise become your daily routine, you will feel a positive change and an uplift in your entire energetic system. All your chakras and your subtle bodies will align.

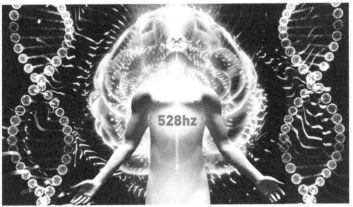

The Lovetuner connects your exhale to the 528hz DNA Repair Frequency

The Lovetuner supports the transformation of all energetic blockades and accumulated old energy in your physical, mental, emotional, and spiritual body. After a 60-day routine, it becomes a part of yourself. Like everything you do with compassion, be open to the possibility that a much faster process might occur. Tuning instantly shows you where your conflicts are located.

Everything that is not in tune with you comes to the surface to be transformed. You tune into your system, and as you tune you strengthen the connection to who you are and to the light inside of you. You reach self-empowerment.

Everything that comes your way from the outside is a mirror of your inner world. Your frequency attracts whatever frequency you are sending out. This is the law of attraction.

"Who looks outside, dreams. Who looks inside, awakens."
—C.G. Jung

Tuning is a great tool to master your life. The Lovetuner connects you to the 528 Hz magical miracle frequency and guides you, showing you where you made compromises or lied to yourself to live in a pretentious harmony.

Whatever is deep down in yourself and is not in tune will come to the surface and needs to be addressed. On your journey, your soul wants you to evolve, and the more insight you get, the more you will be capable of solving significant issues. Like changing grades in school, you know on the one hand nothing is easy anymore; it gets more complicated, but on the other hand, you start doing better and better every day.

At one point, you are at the college level, and you master things with ease. Even though your challenges are getting more intense, you know that you have gained all abilities to master those challenges. Your system is in tune, and you can create infinite possibilities for yourself.

It is why the Lovetuner is the ultimate tool for self- empowerment. It becomes one with you, and while tuning on your journey, you recognize that your power can only come from within.

We are all beings that are constantly and permanently making experiences every single moment of our life. As a soul, we create those experiences on a higher level. To learn, evolve, and grow on our journey, we bring them down and manifest them in our daily lives.

Knowing that the Lovetuner has a strong effect on our energetic system, we know that increasing our frequency does not mean we can stick a Band-Aid over unreleased issues that we carry in our system. Our subtle bodies contain unresolved blockages and traumas.

Where do all these experiences get processed and transformed? Let us be aware of the following facts: Just because we no longer think about negative experiences in our so-called mental body, it does not mean that they have automatically disappeared from our emotional life, our emotional body. The good news: We all can release current or old blockades and traumas from our subtle body system, the so-called aura. This is where the Lovetuner comes in.

While we are tuning, we increase our energy frequency and our vibration. Tuning brings out the positive sides in us. It is why we feel peaceful and in harmony with ourselves and our environment every time we tune in.

On the other hand, tuning also reveals our inner shadows, which we would like to transform to achieve a better quality of life. Here the Lovetuner helps us by essentially supporting the transformation of disruptive factors such as blockages and negative memories in our energetic system.

Let's be aware of how valuable the work of the Lovetuner is when we tune.

As we tune, negative energy flows out of our system, and we feel transformed, balanced, and lifted. Our vibration raises. Returning to the self-empowerment we talked about earlier, the true beauty is you are doing all this yourself. Fully self-empowered and fully aware of the fact that creation needs no understanding by the brain; it happens by heart.

You do not need to understand, you do not need to study, and your mental body can never reach the dimension of your heart. All you need to do is use your Lovetuner to become a self-empowered being. Be your own guru.

Sometimes when I reflect on my journey, I am very humbled

and grateful that my urge to reach a deeper level of understanding of life has brought me to the point of being introduced to the 528 Hz frequency. He who is in search of understanding will finally find the truth.

For me, truth meant finding what was in perfect resonance with me and my divine plan as a soul, finding my mission and higher purpose to serve mankind.

On the other hand, after starting Lovetuner with my partners, not getting any support from them, and finding myself left alone with tons of work and more or less running a company and a mission by myself, I started to doubt.

At that point in my life and in my professional career, I was ready to exit, proceed with my art projects, and travel the world kitesurfing.

Nevertheless, I had no other choice than to fulfill my mission. Every day tuning and experiencing a stronger divine connection made me understand that the Lovetuner is much more than a product. In life, you can have a job, a career, or a calling, and the Lovetuner mission is my calling.

Lovetuner Seminar Switzerland 2019

It is a global movement that can heal the world, and it is my duty to help bring peace and happiness back to this planet and replace darkness, which has been here for such a long time, with light and unconditional love.

Deep down in my heart, I strongly felt the calling to connect hearts and build a global community of oneness to overcome all boundaries and unite all hearts. Becoming aware of all this, I never doubted a minute of my lifetime investment in the Lovetuner mission.

For a couple of years, it was beautiful to see that things started to shift positively in many different aspects of my life. On the outside, I was living a beautiful everyday life. I had two happy and healthy children, a beautiful wife, a successful career with an international network, and a life of travel and leisure. All things seemed to be excellent, measured by our society's standards.

It is what my own experience shows with the Lovetuner. It simply doesn't stop on a superficial level. Slowly but steadily, it goes into your more profound levels and reveals everything you don't want to look into. By tuning into the 528 Hz frequency, you consciously send love into everything you don't want to look at.

Based on your good intentions, you think you can bend the cosmic law of frequency and vibration. No matter how much love you are sending yet not achieving true harmony, a transformational process is not completed.

In my case, I realized that I was not happy with the superficial, even though it meant leaving my comfort zone and making a significant change.

Sometimes life puts you in a position where you have to

decide to either repair or reinvent what is not in harmony with yourself. It is like getting a bill from the repair shop for fixing or servicing your car.

Your first thought might be, wow, this is an expensive bill. Yet, when you get comfortable using the Lovetuner, you will realize that this car is you in your own life, and this is worth all the effort and the investment.

You will realize that the Lovetuner is your divine repair shop. It gives you clear and neutral feedback on what you can or have to repair or improve in your life.

First, on a physical level, by starting to breathe right, you are calming your nervous system, reaching a meditative state of mind, and reaching heart coherence. Further, you will experience the meditative side, and in my case, it replaced my meditation ritual and became the best daily mindfulness routine I have ever had.

Lovetuner Yoga Session Malibu 2014

CHAPTER X

THE LOVETUNER AND MINDFULNESS

Mindfulness or mental hygiene is key for a clean system. Eight years ago, I came out of my yearly cleanse I had done for eight weeks and no longer felt any resonance with alcohol or anything that would disconnect me from the source.

Even though I never had an addictive personality or had any reason to change my lifestyle, the Lovetuner encouraged me to keep going and demanded purification. I knew that if I wanted to be the change I wanted to see in the world, I would have to maintain that initial feeling of shifting things positively. I felt that a profound transformation was the only way to create my future life.

Pushing through with this, I also experienced that when you change on the inside, you will see change on the outside. People in my life changed. A lot of them left, and new people came into my life. Living my life with the Lovetuner simply adjusted everything and everyone that was not meant to raise their frequency together with me.

I must acknowledge the presence of painful experiences on my path, for they compelled me to confront and release that which did not align with higher frequencies and with positive vibrations.

On the other hand, so much love came into my life. My relationship with my kids improved to a level of love and bonding I would have never dreamt of. So many new people who resonated with the new higher frequencies entered my life, people who were searching for a new meaning in life and who would understand that it takes way more than superficial actions like esoterically mainstream practices.

Mindfulness consists of being in the here and now, being consciously present in all activities and thoughts. Body and mind are in harmony. It means to be attentive in a certain way, in the present moment and without judging and prejudice.

This kind of attention promotes awareness, clarity, and openness to the experience of the present moment. When we are fully present in the here and now, we begin to recognize our true being without being trapped in our past or affected by our thoughts about the future.

Suppose we choose to pay attention to ourselves and others with an open mind, without being trapped in our likes and dislikes, good and evil, opinions and prejudices, projections and expectations. In that case, we have the chance to free ourselves from the constraints of the conceptual mind and the prevailing discourses. We see new possibilities. Our

relationships with each other and with the world unfold.

Mindfulness is a practice that helps us to get to a place where we can listen to silence and move out of our heads and into our hearts. Overall it is a practice, not an abstract concept or ideology, of being completely united with life.

Bioresonance and biofrequency testing show that the Lovetuner enhances vital signals up to 90 percent within five minutes of tuning.

Science and studies on mindfulness and heart coherence, as well as HRV in stress medicine and psychophysiology, clearly show the healthy path each of us should explore.

Over the last decades, various biofeedback techniques and devices have been developed to measure heart rate variability. Particular emphasis has been placed on measuring the coupling of heart and respiration to determine the degree of coherence or synchronization between heart rhythm and respiratory rate. Synchronization and chaotic progression of breathing rhythm and heart rate can be visualized visually or acoustically with these biofeedback methods. The pulse is measured with the help of a chest strap or an ear clip, whereby the data is evaluated specially.

It was determined that for reactions as complex as love or gratitude, which are associated with the emotional reaction of joy, a measurable synchronization of the rhythms of heart and respiration (respiratory sinus arrhythmia) occurs.

However, this balance between breathing and heartbeat disappears in reactions such as rush ("stress"), anger, or fear, which are accompanied by an increased release of stress hormones. In the last few years, an increasing amount of research has been conducted in the USA to determine the extent to which coherence of heart and breathing can be trained and to which therapeutic successes can be achieved in different settings. Bio-feedback techniques are used, and in several variations, the aim is to influence the trainees' emotional experience in a targeted manner, either additionally or alternatively.

Extraordinary musical compositions are used, as are breathing techniques, mindfulness exercises, trance inductions, or guided imaginations with a concentration on the heart and breathing in connection with the activation of particularly positive, for example, loving reactions.

Some studies, reviews, and meta-analyses indicate that HRV is reduced in people with mental illness compared to mentally healthy individuals. HRV biofeedback has been used as a coaching method or as a complementary medical method in behaviorally oriented-psychotherapy for quite some time.

According to US studies, depression, heart disease, asthma, anxiety disorders, and insomnia can be favorably influenced. In addition, improving the coherence of breathing and the heart can also help to reduce tension, help to cope with stress and anxiety, and help to react more calmly in everyday life.

HRV biofeedback has been used in workplace health promotion for some time. According to a study published in 2017, HRV biofeedback can also be used to improve athletes' performances.

The National Institutes of Health granted funding to Luskin of Stanford University for research into HRV training for patients with severe heart failure. Patients suffered from shortness of breath, fatigue, edema, and in many cases, also from anxiety and depression.

After six weeks of treatment, the stress level of the group that had learned to use HRV training had decreased by 22 percent and their depression by 34 percent, while the physical condition of walking without shortness of breath had improved by 14 percent. However, no change in HRV was observed.

In the control group, in which conventional agents were used, all of the above indicators had worsened from baseline.

In top-class sports, the training load with HRV is increasingly controlled and managed to avoid overloading. For example, the four New Zealand rowing world champions in 2015 had periodically trained with HRV from day-to-day during the intensive phases before the world championships.

They used the RMSSD (root mean square of the successive differences) as a reference value.

This allows the effect of individual outliers to be minimized mathematically. Since endurance athletes usually already have a very low resting heart rate, the influence of the parasympathetic nervous system is also taken into account.

The journey begins when you first tune, and the only thing you can do to not get through this journey is not to tune. So, if you want to be in tune with yourself if you want to be in tune with your soul, then this is the ultimate thing and the ultimate practice that you can do. And as we all know, we are all connected, and all is one and one is all.

Our higher and collective consciousness has the exact needs we have at the soul level. The light nourishes them, and we know about manifestation in these times of high frequencies in which we live, compared to decades before, that things manifest in a very short time.

It is not that the institutional belief system tells us we are here to fulfill our birthright, and our birthright is to be happy. If you are not happy, you are missing out on your life. You're missing out on your lifetime, and you're missing out on the meaning of your life.

Only you can make yourself happy. As soon as you start doing this, you will realize, you can spread this happiness by keeping your vibration high and not attaching yourself to collective negativity. True happiness cannot be achieved if you are still trapped in an unhealthy belief system.

You know very well that nothing good can come of it. Waiting for negativity to turn into positivity is a waste of time. Negativity must be detached. That is the only way it cannot manifest in our collective consciousness.

By tuning into the love and light and aligning with the 528 Hz frequency, you allow the miracle of positivity to manifest in your life.

Knowing all this, it's a very conscious decision that what is important to you, you have to look into and make those adjustments or that change to stay or become happy.

In my case, the family was number one. But if you see that things are not in harmonious resonance with yourself, then you have to do everything to create a vibrational experience that brings you back into balance. If you raise your frequency, things will continually transform for the better.

Your transformation with an open heart, trusting yourself, and having faith in God will guide you to the path of life you are here for. Just have faith and trust in the process.

Whenever life gives you clear signs, you have to realize that you are not here to suffer. Your soul wants you to live your best, highest, and most divine form of existence. As the creator of your own life, you always have the choice to live your best life. Be aware that your soul will never give up on you. Even if you are not ready to make the change right away and stay in circumstances where you suffer, life will continue to give you choices to change. We call these signs escalation levels. Following is a model showing these escalation levels for a better understanding.

As we navigate through life, we often find ourselves in constantly recurring situations. We often ask ourselves: "Why me" or "Why is this happening again?"

The answer is: Life always wants the best for us and shows us clear signs, so we can evolve from such recurring situations. We call it "evolving processes." So even if you have the feeling that life is kicking your ass, it is never a punishment; it is a reminder to step up and fulfill your soul's purpose. God never punishes us; we cannot handle the free will God gave us in this human experience as a spirit.

We each come to this world with a soul plan that contains all the key data of all incarnations.

The key data refers to what focus the soul chooses to set in all lives, e.g., being a healer, being a servant, being a leader, predominantly female or male incarnations. The soul makes all experiences perfect itself, which means that every soul makes male and female experiences as a human being a victim and a perpetrator at some point, etc. The soul determines these parameters in accordance with the higher self, the karmic council, the lords of time, the blue lodge, and of course in agreement with the Creator or the creation. Besides these key points, everything else in individual incarnations is subject to free will. That is, the human being can have an experience, as they say, early and easy—that would then be an experience exactly according to the soul's plan—or late and expensive, which then would result in corresponding escalation levels. Such a process begins very early in an undesirable life situation and with clear signs. And it can also be finished very quickly if we understand that we are not victims of the circumstances, but the creator of our own lives and can transform or dissolve the recurring events through a clear decision to change and change behavior in daily life.

Most of the time, we are not aware of the signs of life. We tend to overhear and overlook them based on our stressful daily challenges and information overload. Then life has no other chance than to point out to us another time—this time in a more tangible form—to require a change in our patterns and behavior to improve or end the life circumstances, the situation, or possibly the disease accordingly.

We call these symptoms of life escalation levels. In total, there are seven of them. Below is a model of what these escalation levels with different symptoms can look like:

- Escalation level 1: Lack of joy
- Escalation level 2: Catch a cold ("fed up" with something or someone)
- Escalation level 3: Flu, broken leg (life gives us time out to think about ourselves or to change)
- Escalation level 4: Chronic complaints, loss of job (a constantly recurring reminder that change is needed)

- Escalation level 5: Heart attack, divorce, bankruptcy (a drastic experience, but reversible)
- Escalation level 6: Cancer, depression, the so-called stroke of fate (here only a 180-degree turn of opinion or behavior is effective)
- Escalation level 7: End of incarnation (between levels 1 and 7, 20 or more years often pass)

The escalation levels show increasing symptomatology. We are challenged not to fight the symptom as usual, but to investigate the root cause. When a creator sets a new root cause, he thereby produces a new effect. Coupled with altered, progressive behavior, the symptoms become redundant and dissolve.

New, constructive behaviors produce the desired results in the here and now and in the future.

"In life, nothing happens by chance or without reason. God does not play dice." —Albert Einstein.

Knowing the escalation levels and fine-tuning your system will help you better address and transform emotional, physical, and mental imbalances.

Now that you know you are guided, and nothing can happen to you, you will give new meaning to the old saying:

"It's all good in the end, and if it's not good yet, it's not the end."

Or:

"You cannot fall lower than in God's hand."

It may sound so simple, but it is so true because we are here to fulfill our birth-given rights to be happy, healthy, and free.

CHAPTER XI

RESONANCE AND HARMONY

When we talk about the Lovetuner and the 528 Hz frequency, we always talk about the so-called love frequency. What is love, and what is our understanding of love? Love, as we know it, refers to the love between couples, between friends, and the love on a common level.

At the time in life when we experience higher love, also called collective love or unconditional love, we, probably for the first time, get an understanding of where the real power of love is within. We learn that unconditional love is the strongest force in our universe. This love is divine, can overcome everything, and conquers all.

I am convinced that the easiest way to connect to this field of unconditional love is by using the power of the Lovetuner. While we are tuning, we open our hearts to that God-given power. Our heart is the gateway to higher love.

It is my main reason to push the Lovetuner mission and spread the knowledge of how everyone on our planet can access this power and use the frequency of love to their benefit and for the higher good of humankind.

Gaining knowledge and getting an understanding of frequency and vibration, we eventually figure out that long before human bodies even touch, your energy already meets on a higher level.

It should not be underestimated, because it is the power of energy that brings you either into a relationship or not. It's a specific frequency, a certain vibration, that even creates the possibility that love will eventually be the energy between two people and let them get into harmony.

So, before you even go to the point of talking about feeling connected, it is essential to be aware of your energy level which creates harmony or disharmony. People usually tend to underestimate the aspect of vibrational energy. When we talk about everything in frequency and vibration, we talk about resonance, which decides if we feel drawn to someone or to whom we are not attracted.

It is exactly the point where using the Lovetuner can shift so much. Because it brings you into tune, it creates a harmonious field around you. It does not mean that everything gets better right away, but what it does is it shows you your frequency and feedback on where you stand and gives you a chance to reach a higher level by using the Lovetuner. You will be lifted up. Tuning elevates your frequency and your vibration.

When people talk a lot about finding their life partner, their soulmate, or however you want to name it, there is a need for a basic understanding of how energy works and how energies flow.

As said above, long before any physical contact happens, the energies need to align on a higher level. When the soul designs its soul plan, it also chooses the people who will help to fulfill that soul plan, and who will make themselves available for certain experiences. This is a complex issue because at the same time these souls who are there to be a part of your plan, they are also make their corresponding experience in their soul plan.

A soul family does not necessarily consist of a human family, that is, on a physical basis. Soul family means all souls which have agreed to make a common experience. Many soul families are united in an association, which is called a monad. Here also experiences are made, which, however in the broader sense do not necessarily serve the individual experience of the soul, but the development of the whole of humanity.

When your frequency aligns with another person, you create romance. The alignment of your vibration is what can create an everlasting bond. True romance transforms over time and will grow with your evolvement.

Be aware you can only meet on a human level when your energy is in harmony on a higher level.

The universal law of harmony says life itself always creates a balance. So, when something is missing, something is added

Lovetuning with your partner elevates your
spiritual connection and strengthens your love bond

by life, and where there is too much, something is distributed
elsewhere. In the end, life itself creates harmony.

Most people understand harmony to mean that everything
remains constant, always in an equal vibration. We often speak
of the so-called everlasting peace. And we believe that harmony
on the outside can make us happy on the inside.

However, precisely the opposite is the case. If we want to
create true harmony, then it is our task to go inside and explore what can be brought into harmony within us. Only when
we are genuinely ready to explore our innermost being and
discover what is out of balance within us, can we then create
the possibility to manifest harmony on the outside.

Our willingness to recognize and transform disharmonies
within us enables completely new insights into a harmonious
life. For when we recognize that we are creators of our own
lives, we know that we must first transform all disharmonies
within ourselves to create real, lasting harmony in the outside
world for ourselves and the world around us.

True harmony means that nothing can throw us off balance because we are resting stable within us. We meet many people who live in a so-called belief harmony. They tell us that their daily rituals consist of various esoteric techniques, and as long as nothing unusual happens their harmony seems to be perfect. However, if our harmony is dependent on everything outside working perfectly, we have not created any real harmony within ourselves. Therefore, if we want to grow beyond our daily rituals and reach a point in life where we are at rest within ourselves, no matter what happens on the outside; then it is important to go inside and reflect and be ready to look at and heal all the inequalities within us. Only then is true harmony possible. The Lovetuner can be a game changer for us towards true harmony. Using it enables us to get an instant deeper look inside ourselves and create a daily easy and fast ritual that supports any transformation within while keeping our inner life on a high frequency and making room for true and lasting harmony. The law of harmony says: As inside, so outside. So, we always have a choice.

When it comes to the next generation, the Lovetuner Foundation is very interested in engaging there. We find it very important for young people to tune in and to be in tune with their emotions, to be in harmony with the bio-field around them. For them, it is easier to adjust their frequencies and stay in tune, which will help them develop a warning system, something like an indicator for good or bad vibes.

This young generation is layer free, and that indicator will support them in staying away from low frequencies such as addictive gaming and other energy-absorbing devices that kill creativity and lead to depression.

When we understand that our universe consists of frequency, vibration, resonance, and harmony, the cosmic order will feel less abstract.

As the scientist Nikola Tesla said: "If you want to find the secrets of the universe, think in terms of frequency and vibration."

Let us take an insight into the cosmic order and universal laws:

The term cosmos originates in the ancient Greek language and means order. The laws that create or regulate this order are also called hermetic principles, spiritual laws, cosmic laws, laws of creation, or laws of life.

These laws are as old as the universe itself. All life happens, acts, and reacts according to these divine laws, which determine and flow through our entire life and all that is. Regardless of whether we know about them or not, we believe in them or not.

There are no coincidences—all events are subject to cosmic laws.

All laws interact with each other; not all are known, but all are equally "important" or equally "valid."

As creators of our life, we always choose to live by the laws and benefit from them or deny their existence and work against our soul's purpose. It is our decision. The laws do not distinguish between "good" and "evil" or "right" or "wrong." They only let appear 1:1 what we have chosen, utterly free of value.

All universal laws vibrate at different frequencies and represent a unique cosmic sound, frequency, and vibration of creation. The Lovetuner is a symbol of universal sound, frequency, and light. To open our hearts and spread love is our mission, the mission of all mankind. The Lovetuner supports this mission and our ability to raise our consciousness and brings our energy into a higher dimension, love, and unity. All is one and one is all.

The Lovetuner and the Universal Law of Love

Love is the strongest force in the universe. Love does not demand anything, it does not condition anything, and it is entirely free. In ancient Greek, we talk about agape as the name for divine love, from soul to soul, unconditional love.

The universal law of love says that we may first love ourselves unconditionally. Because only when we love ourselves true love for other people and all creatures is possible. The degree of self-love determines the love we can give and receive.

Therefore, self-love does not mean being egoistic but treating ourselves, other beings, and everything that is with respect and attentiveness. Through this, we gain confidence in ourselves and achieve self-consciousness.

When we are fully aware of and love ourselves, we send out love and thus go in resonance with the universal love, which can then flow back to us.

The primary prerequisite for this is to raise our vibration. The higher our vibrational frequency is, the easier it is for us to create a positive resonance so that all that we love can flow into our lives.

With the Lovetuner you have the opportunity to always be in the vibration of love and thus automatically attract everything that vibrates in this high frequency of love.

The Lovetuner and the Universal Law of Vibration

Fear is the lowest-vibrational frequency. Love is the highest-vibrational frequency. When you send out resonances out of the vibration of fear, you automatically attract everything that makes you afraid, that keeps you lacking.

When you send out vibrations of resonance from the vibration of love, you automatically attract everything you love and everything that loves you.

You are this resonance body. Imagine you are using the Lovetuner to increase your resonance body, your vibration, and your frequency.

Every time you use the Lovetuner, you raise your vibration into the vibration of love, into the highest vibration that exists in this universe.

That is the vibration of light, to be equalized with the vibration of love.

If you tune in every day, and you do it with joy and with love, then you automatically attract everything in life which is at the highest vibration, which is love.

The affirmation in tuning can be, for example, "I attract everything that I love."

And another thing is essential: Confirm this to the universe. Tell the universe and yourself, your subconscious, "I am good enough."

Because to put on something that you love is only one half of the law, but it also lives in your system, lives in your life; it is important that you know deep inside that "I am good enough."

For example, the affirmation while tuning can be: "I am good enough."

And if that doesn't work perfectly in the beginning, that's not necessarily a bad thing. We are here to practice. We are incarnated on this planet not to be perfect but to practice.

Earth is a playing field where the players practice getting better every day. And you are one of those players. So, if you cannot do everything perfectly on your first try, keep on practicing! The Lovetuner supports you in practicing every single day. So easy, so fast, so effective, and so wonderful.

The Lovetuner allows you to always stay in the vibration of love and automatically attract everything that vibrates at a high frequency.

The Lovetuner and the Universal Law of Resonance of Attraction

Everything occurs according to the cosmic laws, the law of resonance, and the universal law of attraction. The same attracts the same and is strengthened by the same. Unbalanced things repel each other. The higher determines the lower.

We attract what we focus on as the creators of our own life. Fear attracts what we fear. Love attracts what we love. The energy always follows the attention: "I attract everything that scares me." Conversely, "I attract everything that I love."

"You are the creator of your own life. You decide."

With the Lovetuner you have the opportunity to always be in the vibration of love and thus automatically attract everything that resonates with you at this high frequency.

The Lovetuner and the Universal Law of Cause and Effect

The law itself has no decision-making power. It only brings to light 1:1 the effect of what we, as the creator of our own lives, set as the spiritual cause. If a creator establishes a cause, he consistently produces an effect according to the law. The appearance factor is not subject to linear time. This means that the effect that we experience in this life may have been set as the cause in another incarnation and may appear in this life at some so-called escalation level.

In this quality of time, effects can often occur immediately after setting a cause because the increase in the planet's frequency causes a "time acceleration."

Through the Lovetuner you have the opportunity to always be in the vibration of love. If you, as the creator of your own life, set causes that are carried by love, you automatically produce an effect that is carried by love.

The Lovetuner and the Universal Law of Abundance

Material abundance is an expression of the universe. We find this abundance everywhere in our lives, in the smallest cell up to the greatest wonder, our nature, our creation. All life evolves and gives us abundance in abundance. It is our birthright to express this abundance in our lives. An abundance of love, health, freedom, and happiness.

The opposite of abundance is deficiency. A low vibrational frequency accompanies deficiency; abundance corresponds to a high-vibrational frequency. Deficiency is an expression of limited thinking; abundance is the expression of our hearts. Thinking with the heart enables abundance in our entire being.

With the Lovetuner you can always stay in the vibration of love and automatically attract everything that vibrates in this high frequency of abundance. So, abundance can flow easily and freely into your life.

The affirmation during tuning can be, e.g., "I am divine abundance."

The Lovetuner and the Universal Law of Gratitude

Gratitude is the sister of love. Divine humility and gratitude form a wonderful foundation for a richly fulfilling life. Everything for which we are grateful from the bottom of our hearts in our lives comes back to us a thousand times over. Per the spiritual laws, there is always a balance in the universe.

When we send out genuine gratitude as resonance, we

are rewarded with gratitude from the universe. To be grateful without expectation—even for an unpleasant learning experience—means to acknowledge the principles of the laws of life and thus attain heightened consciousness in resonance. As creators of our own lives, we always determine the time factor ourselves.

With the Lovetuner you have the opportunity to always stay in the vibration of love and thus automatically attract everything that vibrates in this high frequency of gratitude.

The affirmation during tuning can be, e.g.: "I am divine gratitude."

The Lovetuner and the Universal Law of Blessing

The law is beyond any religion, it is not reserved to any office, and every human being can and may use it for their own blessing and for the blessing of others and all that is.

To bless a person from the power of the heart means to create a respectful and sincere connection from soul to soul. Since there are no reservations or resentments between souls, the one whom I bless with a sincere heart is blessed similarly. Do everything for your best, highest, and most divine. If it also serves the good of the community, it must be blessed and successful according to all spiritual laws.

It makes sense, for example, to bless conflict situations.

Physically you can bless an organ (not the disease) or the entire body.

Whether material or immaterial, the attitude of the heart is decisive.

With the Lovetuner you have the opportunity to always stay in the vibration of love and thus automatically attract everything that vibrates in this high frequency of blessing.

While you are tuning, your affirmation can be, for example: "I am blessing myself, and I am blessing you."

The first time those laws were written down was by the ancient Egyptian Master Thoth, also known as the divine writer. These records are known as the so-called Emerald Tablets. In ancient Greek mythology, he is called Hermes Trismegistos. It is the reason why they are called The 7 Hermetic Principles.

The Emerald Tablet of Thoth

The 7 Hermetic Principles

1. The Principle of Spirituality - The all is the spirit; the universe is spiritual. All material things develop from the spiritual. A spiritual event preceded all visible events.

2. The Principle of Analog - As above, so below. As on the inside, so on the outside.

3. The Principle of Vibration - Nothing ever rests; everything is in motion, and everything oscillates. The law of resonance is the law of transmission of energy. Every vibration transmits the energy acting in it to every bodily oscillation with the same vibration.

4. The Principle of Polarity - Everything is twofold; everything is polar, and everything has two opposites. Opposites are identical by nature, only different in their degree. ALL truths are only half-truths because they can be seen from two sides.
5. The Principle of Rhythm - Everything flows. Greek: Panta Rhei. Everything has its tides. Everything rises and falls. Rhythm smoothens out. The swing of the pendulum to the right is the measure for the swing to the left.
6. The Principle of Cause and Effect - Every cause has its effect; every effect has its cause. "Coincidence" is only a term for an unrecognized law.
7. The Principle of Gender - Gender is in everything; everything has its masculine and feminine principles. Gender manifests on all levels.

For a long time in my life I was unaware of the consequences of casual sex, and even when I was deep into the Lovetuner journey, I still didn't fully understand the drama I was experiencing around me as a consequence of careless use of sexual energy.

By being more mindful, it became apparent that the exchange of sexual energy has a huge impact. If a person carries guilt, shame, or trauma, you can energetically absorb that. It's like going around and plugging your phone into random people's computers and downloading their files. If there are corrupt files in their system, you also download them. Sex is a sacred act and should be treated as such.

All relationships create energetic cords. Sexual relationships create strong energy bands that can affect your emotional, mental, spiritual, and even physical health. Every time we choose to have a casual sexual relationship with someone, whether it is even just for one night, we create energy connections with that person.

Casual sex is not a "bad" thing, it is simply an experience, but it has consequences. One of the most powerful energies that people have at their disposal is sexual energy. Kundalini is our divine life energy, and at that moment, when we physically connect our body with that of another person, we automatically connect on much deeper levels.

Pay attention to whom you are sharing your intimate energy with. Intimacy on this level connects your aural energy with the aural energy of the other person. No matter how insignificant one thinks they are, these powerful connections leave spiritual fragments, especially in people who do not practice any kind of purification, physical, emotional, or otherwise.

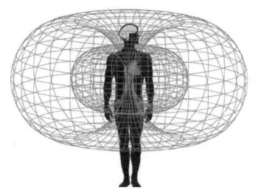

The Heart is more powerful than the Brain
The Heart is about 100,000 times stronger electrically & up
to 5,000 times stronger magnetically than the brain.

The more we interact intimately with someone, the deeper
the connection and the more their aura is connected to yours.
Imagine the confused aura of someone who sleeps with several people and carries around these multiple energies with
them. What they may not realize is that others are sensing this
energy as a result of us looking at them, and in this way, we
repel positive and negative energy into our lives.

Never sleep with someone you don't want to be with. Whatever is in the other person's field, such as their thoughts and
unresolved emotions, can become entangled with your field.
It is standard for people to have casual sex while consuming
alcohol. It is a bigger problem because alcohol lowers the
natural protection of the energy field, and one is now even
more susceptible to absorbing disharmonious energies from
the other person.

Physical contact between two people mixes their auras
and energy fields. Usually these states are only temporary, but
there can be continued unresolved energy which can manifest
physically, emotionally, mentally, and spiritually.

On a physical level, unresolved and unknown physical energy from the other person is left over in one's system after having casual sex. Sometimes it can lead to physical illness, depending on the physical condition of the sex partners.

On an emotional level, unresolved and unknown emotional energy from the other person would be the energetic form that is left over in one's system after having casual sex. Sometimes it can lead to emotional discomfort, depending on the emotional condition of the sex partners.

On a mental level, unresolved and unknown mental energy from the other person would be the energetic form that is left over in one's system after having casual sex. Sometimes it can lead to mental confusion, depending on the state of mind of the sex partners.

On a spiritual level, unresolved and unknown spiritual energy from the other person would be the energetic form that is left over in one's system after having casual sex. Sometimes it can lead to spiritual disorientation.

After these encounters, you might be left with thoughts and emotions that are not yours, but because the energy is affecting you, you will eventually identify with this pattern and further energize these mental and emotional states which energize you. As soon as you become intimate with someone, you merge with their energy. Also, it doesn't matter if it is cyber or physical sex. Whenever you are intimate with someone, you absorb their energy. Also, they absorb your energy. If you interact closely with uplifting, positive, and loving people, that positive energy will uplift you.

If you interact with unstable, depressive, pessimistic, and negative people, this negative energy can put you down.

So, if you have ever had casual sex with multiple partners, it would be wise to cleanse those energies and cut the cords. If one night of casual sex can have this effect, imagine what consequence years of sexual intimacy with an ex-lover, partner, or spouse could lead to.

SACRED   ENERGY   EXCHANGE

Remember that sex is neither "good" nor "bad." Sex is a powerful and pleasurable experience, so be wise to implement your judgment when deciding whom to share sex with.

The lack of freedom in the system we are living in corrupted our human relations and took love out of the equation.

This quote from Krishna Murti brings it to the point for me, and therefore I am sharing it below:

"Why has sex become so extraordinarily important? I think this is a question that must be faced and answered, not evaded. Why have we given such extraordinary importance to it? Is it that we are not essentially free?

"We are not free, even though you may think we are —we are caught, trapped by religions, education, fears, and so on, and we have become a prisoner to all this. So, the only escape is through sex, and so sex and pleasure become very important. The richer you are, the more extravagant your pleasures. And human beings, right throughout the world and through centuries, have pursued pleasure; when pleasure becomes dominant in life, love goes. One has to understand the nature of desire and pleasure, not condemn it."

I got a lot of feedback from friends and clients that integrated the Lovetuner into their sex life to not only physically connect, but also at the same time to connect in this frequency field and experience harmonic resonance.

To be in a higher frequency allows you, besides the physical pleasure, to experience a heartfelt connection on a higher level.

CHAPTER XII

THE SPIRITUAL REVOLUTION

Let us face it, at the beginning of the pandemic and the lockdown, it depended on how totalitarian and fascist governments and local politicians dealt with this matter, either with a human approach or a fascist approach.

It affected the country, and the place where you lived, depending on how you experienced it with your government or local politicians. It was not intended to do any good, but it gave us as individuals time to reflect and a renewed connection with nature.

It was sad to see that so many did not take the opportunity to go within and change things in their lives for the better. Many began to numb themselves and distract themselves with alcohol and drugs, etc.

At the same time, it was nice to see how forgiving nature is, and how clean the air and oceans became in a very short time. Our urge to return to so-called normality ended up continuing in an unhealthy pattern. We plunged right into a world that became even more complex and unhealthy.

Whatever mindfulness routine you have, whatever you do to keep yourself sane, needs to be profoundly integrated into your lifestyle. You cannot on one hand see and acknowledge what is right and what is wrong, and then do the wrong, opposite thing. If your vibration is aligned with the universal laws, then it is your absolute duty to keep your frequency high, regardless of what is going on in the world around you.

Everything began with sound and vibration; we were just no longer aware of this cosmic law and our longing for harmony. Returning to the awareness and knowledge that everything is frequency and vibration will change our human experience as a soul.

On the contrary, in our modern society everything possible is done to bring the individual and all of humanity into disharmony. Any man-made disharmonious frequency that serves a repressive, restrictive, and controlling system is deliberately used to exert an unpleasant vibrational effect on people.

Fear and anxiety are the predominant frequencies used to reprogram and condition people to keep them at a lower level of consciousness. Anyone who is at a low frequency and in a state of fear is easily manipulated. In this state of consciousness, we are disconnected from our higher self and the source.

Over time, fear, anger, hatred, and envy have replaced our birthright of love, freedom, abundance, and happiness. For people, harmonious frequencies such as the feeling of gratitude and love have been forgotten, and instead, their implemented negative frequencies feel familiar. In this disharmonious environment, negative frequencies can be used for domination and manipulation in all systems worldwide.

The Lovetuner does a great service to humanity because it is a device that connects the inner world, which we call spirituality, with the outer world, which is science. That is what you are experiencing. It connects the physical body with the subtle body.

The quote that the glass is either half full or half empty has always been considered a matter of attitude. The Lovetuner gives you a new perspective on a deeper meaningful and spiritual level beyond your attitude.

It does not mean that the Lovetuner will solve your problems, but it will allow you to change your perception to where the solution is already right in front of you.

This solution is in harmony and resonance with you. You can choose how you want to perceive things. Life is not happening to you, but for you. Indeed, you will be stuck in not-so-pleasant situations from time to time.

If you take a moment and reflect, you will always find a reason behind everything. Some circumstances have helped you grow, learn, reflect, develop, and made you stronger.

Whatever it is, you always have the choice to see unfavorable circumstances as a learning process and thus make the best out of every situation and your life.

If you don't like your current situation, you can either detach from it or decide to look at it from a different perspective. When we talk about frequency and vibration, it means raising your frequency. In an environment with high vibration, you feel good. In an environment with low vibration, you feel bad.

What is the easiest way to raise your vibration? The answer is simple: Connect to a higher frequency. Breathwork with the Lovetuner connects your exhalation to the 528 Hz frequency and you feel the love on a cellular level.

One of my favorite quotes about energy is: "When tension goes, energy flows."

I live by it, and every morning and every second of the day I get another chance to create the life I want. In the end, it's all about the journey and having fun along the way. So "One Journey" is a symbol for all our journeys. The key to life is happiness; that's your birthright. Happiness is a very high frequency, and that is what we strive for.

In a higher collective consciousness, everything gravitates toward unity and oneness. Separation and polarity have taken us far away from this and distracted us even more from it in our time.

We can only expect change on the outside if we change on the inside. Unfortunately, corporate power is influencing the global political situation, leading us to the systematic destruction of humanity on all levels: economically, morally, and spiritually. This disconnection has made us blind and paralyzed. We are watching the pollution and destruction of Mother Earth. The systematic abuse of religion, race, and gender leads to more and more polarity. By falling for this manipulation, humanity is moving further and further away from unity and harmonious coexistence. We need to connect in the field of unity and overcome polarity, as Rumi says, "Out beyond the ideas of wrongdoing and right doing, there is a field. I will meet you there."

The system that is destroying us does not allow us to live a better and happier life. Healing on a collective level will not be possible if we continue to cling to a political solution. There is only one solution: a spiritual revolution.

Things can only change from within. No one can lie to themselves. Purity and authenticity are the only medicines that can wake up a numbed society. People are forced to get out of their comfort zone, tune in to a higher frequency and overcome bad habits to keep their system pure.

This is the key to helping manifest the Golden Age on a three- dimensional level, which already exists in the fifth dimension. The Golden Age is a term from ancient mythology and is now used in the Aquarian Age for the concept of the state of consciousness after ascension. The Golden Age refers to the primal peaceful phase of humanity before the emergence of civilization, considered the ideal state, into which we are gravitating towards again after the fall of Atlantis 12,000 years ago. Since the birth of our planet, there have been five Golden Ages, and currently we are preparing for the sixth Golden Age, which was initiated in 2012 and will come into effect from the year 2032 as described in the Mayan calendar. An era is called golden because the land and everything on it has a golden aura. The new era is supposed to bear typical features of the mythical Golden Age: an abundance of blessings of nature, peace of animals, and an earth that provides all the food needed by itself and thus eliminates agriculture, seafaring, and trade. Whatever is needed creates itself at the very moment and dissolves itself afterward. Thus there is no more lack and no overproduction. Abundance always arises exactly at the moment in which there is use for it. These details let us recognize that this was not meant metaphorically, but concretely and is. That is, everything creates itself from itself. The state of consciousness of mankind is at a point where it is recognized that all is one and one is all. All boundaries are dissolved. The ego has not died, but has dissolved into the higher self and humanity has realized that divinity exists in all that is.

Lower motivations such as ill will, greed, etc., and feelings of fear have been transformed into divine faith. Love, respect, and mindfulness are the vehicles of higher consciousness.

In ancient times, this was called the paradisiacal state. Spiritually, we as humans have returned to the consciousness of oneness.

The Lovetuner is the perfect device to connect to a higher level and the field of love. In this field of love, we can recreate and overcome systems that do not serve us. The people who are in these systems will change and will realize that the system no longer serves them.

It does not serve their children; it will not serve their grand-children.

The Lovetuner Mission is to unite all hearts to restructure the system and bring a more loving togetherness.

No one must live in poverty now. Everywhere we go, there is abundance. We're not talking about socialism or communism, or any type of political structure.

We live in this world where we believe that money equals wealth, but money is only one form of wealth. There are so many other forms of wealth like kindness, gratitude, community, happiness, or stillness of mind.

Overall, there is only one world in which we live, and with it, we affect an entire universe.

Everything is interconnected, everything conditions each other and interacts with one another.

We are all one. We are creators and all our thoughts and actions influence everything that is, ourselves, the entirety of humanity, our planet, and the whole universe because we are a part of it.

Each of our cells contains all information about the entire universe.

Jesus said, "Whatever you did to the least, you did to me." The hermetic laws say as above, so below, as inside, so outside. The microcosm corresponds to the macrocosm and vice versa.

Our awareness is maturing, and it is starting to manifest on our planet that we are all one, and one is all.The 528 Hz frequency will help us to overcome low consciousness systems and restructure them in a nonviolent way. Because it is the key to the heart. The heart is the place where our decisions should be made.

I have asked this many times in this book: What is our journey, what are we talking about? We are talking about shifting from our heads into our hearts. That is the only place where decisions can be made. Decisions that can save the world, that can make this world a better place, and that overall will help us heal internally and externally.

Nothing can be pushed under the carpet anymore. Political correctness is not the solution and not the answer to calm people down. It is an entirely made-up structure that brings even more polarity. As it simply goes too far in one direction, it will swing back the other way.

We must act to catch this pendulum and bring it back into balance. The spikes of craziness that have nothing to do with reality, nothing to do with humanity, need to be toned down because they add to all the confusion and all the manipulation that people have been bombarded with and had layered on for so long. Here and now is the chance for each of us to step into the responsibility we have to our collective to ignite the light as light workers, as light beings, or as keepers of the light.

In the past, I have made false compromises with myself. What the Lovetuner taught me was not always comfortable because it releases blockades and confronts you with unsolved patterns and your deepest inner longings. It shows you in an unapologetic way your current vibration and what is in true resonance with yourself. All emotions are related to a certain frequency. A lot of different spiritual practices or emotional guidance charts are supposed to help you to reach the so-called flow state. Our mind understands those, and we relate to positive emotions, and we try to avoid low-frequency emotions. Regardless of the practice, instant integration on a cellular level only happens with the Lovetuner.

Things change for the better when you steadily and constantly tune in and align yourself with the 528 Hz frequency because then change will happen over time. This sustainable and lasting change happens on a cellular level. You don't need to do much else, everything will make sense and begin to flow to you effortlessly.

The Lovetuner is a wonderful tool in its purest form. As darkness cannot exist in the light, low-vibrational and ego-driven feelings cannot exist in this frequency. Transforming your ego into your higher self means authenticity in its highest form. When you are authentic, you are in harmony with yourself. When I started to replace my meditation routine with lovetuning, the Lovetuner and connecting to the 528 Hz frequency showed me clearly which emotions are in resonance with my core being. It restructured my life on many levels, especially my private life.

All the negative feelings I was dealing with such as anger, frustration, and mainly confusion, fell off me and I started to realize that this is not me; it was only a construct from outside that had an impact on me.

The Lovetuner sharpened my awareness and slowly but steadily I changed, I changed my frequency and things that had been interesting for me at one point had become obsolete.

This willingness to change for the better is the only thing that can bring us together. We cannot hold on to something that is not in resonance with our journey.

We must step out of this matrix and peel away all layers of confusion, lies, falsehoods, and all toxic constructs that distract us from our true values. Reflecting on our true values leads us to authenticity.

Why do we destroy our planet? We are doing it for too long. We have seen what we did to this planet and there is no excuse to continue with this destruction. We must address it and do everything in our power to save and protect it.

Everyone who uses a Lovetuner and connects to the 528 Hz frequency develops a deeper understanding and a stronger connection to Mother Earth. The 528 Hz frequency can do miracles for humanity and our planet. We heard a lot of things about the Sixties, the hippie era, the Age of Aquarius, and how the world was going to change for the better through love.

Some people made fun of it, and for many, the wish is the father of the thought. Some things never came to pass as they were prophesied.

Many years later, we now understand that we should not wait for love from the outside, but that we can generate it within ourselves and then spread it to the world. In the long run, we will succeed only if we revolutionize the structures in our society that do not serve humanity and life in its purest form. Not with weapons, but with love.

I grew up in a socialist system in Austria, with central economic planning and state regulations.

What we understand by the so-called American Dream was never an option in Austria.

Entrepreneurship is often associated with political parties, and the majority of people still need to explore their economic options. They relied on governmental handouts that were disproportionate to the high taxes.

You were curtailed in your freedom, you were curtailed in your ability to express yourself for many years. The educational system was much better than the one in the United States, but a huge goal in the Austrian system is to make you an obedient citizen.

To discuss religion, race, or politics based on manipulated and corrupted mass media feels to me like opioids given to the masses to numb their senses and to keep them distracted from a complex international system that exploits humanity and takes away even more freedom.

Recognizing this matrix makes it even more evident that self- empowerment and a spiritual revolution is the only solution to overcome this man-made suffering, caused by the systematic disconnect of humans and the continuous destruction of our planet.

What the Lovetuner does for you is self-empowerment. Hoping that political leaders, who are operating in this toxic system, will help humanity is sheer stupidity. The responsibility lies in each of us, in our educational system and in the corporate world.

The Lovetuner program to introduce mindfulness into the corporate world showed that successful corporations in the United States and Europe had positive changes within their corporate structures and ended up with more productive management and happier employees in general.

CHAPTER XIII

THE LOVETUNER AND "CONNECTING SPIRIT AND BUSINESS"

The application of the Lovetuner creates and supports mindfulness in the corporate world.

It leads to many decisive advantages:

Atmosphere in the Company

The Lovetuner creates a relaxed working environment through good vibes. As a result, it reduces conflict potential and creates a better communication level.

The Lovetuner can take out any tension in the everyday entrepreneurial life with its daily challenges in a targeted and timely manner. With the Lovetuner, tension and smoldering conflicts are already cleared or smoothed out in advance.

The high vibration generated by the Lovetuner means high consciousness, good cooperation, and empathic people. Employees who feel comfortable and belong to the company experience less stress and are generally more confident and relaxed.

Top Level

Tuned entrepreneurs, managers, and executives are more confident, relaxed, balanced, communicative, and therefore more successful. It makes them better role models and motivators. Using the Lovetuner on the executive floors eliminates the classical stress factors. Burnout and other typical clinical pictures, such as heart and circulation problems, high blood pressure, etc., among managers can be prevented.

The use of the Lovetuner during business meetings creates a relaxed and harmonious atmosphere. As a result, meetings become more productive, more communicative, and give more pleasure. Where joy is created, creativity can unfold easier, goals can be reached faster, and results can be achieved more clearly.

Teamwork

Team-building is supported and encouraged by the empathy that develops. The Lovetuner, as a "connecting element," creates a "we" feeling in a very simple way. The desired affiliation (socialization) within the team is supported and promoted.

Different attitudes, views, and opinions are communicated neutrally and attentively through the high vibration generated by the Lovetuner. Satisfied teams and employees create greater goals in less time through a productive and, at the same time, relaxed working atmosphere.

Health

The Lovetuner strengthens and supports the immune system. The targeted breathing exercise with the Lovetuner increases lung volume. The 528 Hz frequency harmonizes the water molecules in the body and activates the parasympathetic nervous system, which leads to a state of relaxation within a few breaths with the Lovetuner.

This state of relaxation (the parasympathetic nervous system) reduces stress factors and prevents burnout and other stress disorders.

Relaxed employees are healthier, with fewer absences and sick days. Healthy people make companies future-oriented and successful.

By tuning, break times are turned into so-called mini- vacations and are thus innovative and optimally designed. The "Lovetuner Break" immediately leads to more relaxation, fresh energy, new motivation, and creativity.

It helps to get out of daily and professional stress situations quickly and effectively, and to react calmly to every new challenge.

A healthy and sensible rhythm for reducing stress consists of the following:

An essential aspect is the easy handling of the Lovetuner. It is always within reach and can be used quickly, effectively, and efficiently anywhere.

Research

HRV-Biofeedback has been used in workplace health promotion for some time.

Bioresonance test measurements after using the Lovetuner showed up to a 90-percent improvement in vital functions.

The 528 Hz frequency generated by the Lovetuner can positively influence water cell clusters and support the elimination of toxins. Water that is bundled in a hexagonal shape is of incredible importance for our DNA's structure and health.

Productivity and workflow

Respect, appreciation, well-being, and health of employees are essential to increase a company's productivity.

Happy and balanced people are more productive, creative, and focused, and achieve their goals through better sales. The use of the Lovetuner in "Lovetuner-Breaks" supports concentration and, thus, performance. It is the people who make companies successful.

Fewer divergences create a better workflow, a decisive factor in companies.

Corporate Values

Honesty, integrity, sustainability, respect, and employee orientation are recognized, perceived, and supported as authentic by sovereign leaders and satisfied employees.

Within the range of relationship management between customers and suppliers, especially in sales, different (negatively grown) mental concepts in customer and supplier contact can be prevented using the Lovetuner.

As a result, negotiations and sales talks are more relaxed, easygoing, and attentive, which naturally positively affects the company's success.

Corporate Culture

Modern and future-oriented companies and entrepreneurs place people at the center of entrepreneurial thinking and action. Both employees and managers identify more strongly with the company through solid and authentic corporate values, and the corporate culture, which plays a decisive role both internally and externally, improves significantly.

The importance of company culture research is demonstrated by HAYS Canada's "What People Want" report from 2017, which focuses on the most critical aspects of company culture: The Shopify company is receiving much attention for its corporate culture, often focusing on the perks such as Apple technology, free food, and lavish offices. The company also boasts strong cross-departmental communication and collaboration, numerous career opportunities, and a culture of appreciation.

The results show that perks and amenities do not primarily influence employees and applicants.

A nice office may be a bonus, but no top candidate would stay or apply for a company position without the key cultural pillars of communication, leadership, and work-life balance.

Mindfulness in the Corporate World

Mindfulness and appreciation have become a topic in the business world. The combination of science, mindfulness, and leadership achieves significant results in terms of strengthening employees' team-oriented focus and commitment. In addition, mindfulness practice positively changes mental functions, helps resolve conflicts, and supports focus attention.

Numerous studies on Mindfulness-Based Stress Reduction (e.g., Forbes, Kalapa Leadership Academy) indicate that participants who practice mindfulness are significantly better able to regulate stress and feel less tense and burdened.

In objective attention tests, clear improvements can be seen. An increasing number of companies are showing social responsibility and integrating this type of training. Mindfulness plays a comprehensive role in management. Managers who have access to their leadership competencies in any situation achieve precise, sustainable, and value-adding results.

The Lovetuner offers an effortless way to practice mindfulness through deep breathing exercises. It connects your breathing with a soft, audible sound and the frequency of 528 Hz—the universal frequency of love.

For the individual employee, regular mindfulness practice achieves a goal-oriented alignment and focus. Joint tuning creates connecting, communicative elements in companies, the feeling of belonging, solidarity, and team spirit.

The added value of using the Lovetuner in a business context is obvious. There has never been an easier and more accessible tool to implement the daily requirements and tasks with all of a business's bandwidth and diversity.

CHAPTER XIV

INTUITION

The only form to receive information that is valuable for our lives and enables us to understand creation is intuition.

In our society, old, channeled knowledge received from the divine source got picked up by the so-called spiritual leaders and self-declared gurus. This ancient knowledge is given to humankind to understand that we are all part of the cosmos. Studying this knowledge leads the way to independence and freedom.

This channeled pure knowledge got recycled and intellectually purposely complicated by self-help authors, life coaches, and many spiritual online platforms. It concludes that spirituality can only be experienced intellectually, consciously confusing people seeking answers and making it impossible to activate and listen to their emotional intelligence.

Living a mind-driven life, where intellect rules over emotions, can turn everything into meaningless junk. My mission with the power of the Lovetuner is to empower people to go from their heads into their hearts and help them to achieve a pure channel that allows them to trust their intuition fully.

Interview with Sigmar Berg Malibu 2022

I was never intellectually interested in guidance books but always interested in the pure expression of life and science. Pseudo-spirituality, fortune tellers, horoscopes, and other in-corporated esoteric nonsense never resonated with me. Also, letting the ego die, which spiritual people seem to be obsessed with, is not in resonance with the divine creation, and it places you in a position of being at war with yourself.

The ego that hinders us from letting natural intuition happen is not supposed to die; it can only dissolve in our higher self.

How can you overcome your ego if you are not in resonance with yourself in the first place?

Same as breaking with old habits like alcohol or drugs or any other addiction. It is not possible on a solely mind-based decision or with an unsustainable radical therapy. It only gives you temporary relief and is not integrated on a cellular level.

It is essential to change the root cause and fill the void with a new, stronger, meaningful life purpose.

My first awareness about the journey of mankind and where we are coming from and where we are going to was in South America at a young age. By traveling the world, I experienced different cultures and met powerful indigenous shamans.

Back then, I first felt the power of the heart and silence beyond the spoken word. The Lovetuner is beyond all blah blah blah and gifts you with this exact profound understanding of Mother Nature and our journey through time and space.

When you travel, you meet many people who are engaged in spirituality. Friends of mine were also on this path. Deep down, I always knew that spirituality was something that interested me. Just how spirituality is used and distorted by many people never resonated with me.

Using spirituality as an excuse to escape from reality, to not be in control of one's life, or as a self-announced guru to make other people dependent on oneself seemed absurd to me.

Authentic spiritual teachers never tell you what to do; they guide you on your path to finding your way and solution. For this very reason, God gave us our free will.

Also, all the superficial talk about it, especially from people who did precisely the opposite in their lives of what they talked about in public, made me look at the subject very critically.

The real reason spirituality still feels so abstract to many people is the misinterpretation of many genuine and authentic divine messages. Take, for example, the statement attributed to Jesus: one must turn the other cheek to the enemy. On the surface, that would mean you must put up with everything and be a victim to be a good person.

Here a classic misinterpretation takes place. This statement means that we should give the other person a second chance. It makes us responsible people, not a victim. Nonviolence does not mean our hands are tied and that we must agree to everything. Love does not sugarcoat; love is real.

Furthermore, real love means we have the right to say no where we mean no. It is what a loving person does — knowing their boundaries and showing you that your freedom ends where theirs begins.

When we take responsibility for our lives, we address and solve things. Therefore, there are better solutions than the passive-aggressive way of solving any matter.

Intuitively I felt that there was higher knowledge in me, even if I could not explain it with my mind then. However, in my spiritual body and down to my cellular level, things were very clear to me regarding my journey.

Today I see things as they are, entirely without judgment. Some people make clever speeches about spirituality and are adulated by others for it. Then, some genuinely spiritual people know their mission and dedicate their lives to it without much blah blah. These are the people who truly serve humanity.

Years later, when Lovetuner was already established and we had started branching out, I was introduced to Anne Wolnik. Anne has been a successful leadership management coach and therapist for over 30 years. She developed several patented methods to help people simultaneously live prosperous, grounded, and spiritual lives.

Anne is a medium for the universal energy called "Victory." She became a team rider for Lovetuner. From the beginning, it was clear that we would work together on the mission.

Sigmar Berg and Anne Wolnik Malibu 2020

Later, we also agreed to work on this book together. Our values regarding spirituality are in agreement regarding the fact that staying on a mental level is outdated in these times. The only thing that can make a difference in spirituality is lived daily. Only the emotional level brings about a change in us and in all of humanity.

We talked about the fact that, based on my previous experiences, I am very critical of the whole subject. It was not meant disrespectfully at all; for me, the subject of channeling was very abstract. Anne explained more about it, and at some point, I said, yes, I would like to experience it.

The way Anne teaches is very different in every way from what is offered in the spiritual sector. What she does is she doesn't show you anything. She lets you see. That's a very different experience.

Because many people say, "Oh, I was there, I got this channel and this message, and I got this fortune teller," whatever you want to call it. However, it feels like someone is telling you a story or explaining the movie they just saw in the theater, and you are not experiencing it yourself.

With Anne's teachings, and the exercises we did, and most importantly the patented method of reconnecting with the soul and our compatible energy, it is like you are not even watching your movie; it's like you are the director of your movie, you are the protagonist, you're literally in the movie.

Therefore, it is something far beyond an experience that someone else is telling you.

Approaching it this way made sense to me and is consistent with what the Lovetuner does: you create the frequency within you, unaffected by what someone on the outside is doing for you or telling you.

To return to where I had just started, I did this training with Anne, which fit so well with my journey because all I had before was with my intuition. My intuition has always been good.

Now with channeling, which by the way, is the highest form of intuition, my intuition has grown into its highest form. So, what channeling does is it brings out your intuition again. You start to trust your intuition. And that's what we've all forgotten. Living life by being guided by your intuition brings essential benefits. First, you gain a deep understanding of the cosmos, and your values shift to seeing life as precious as it is. Your decisions become crystal clear, and your life path unfolds right before you.

Living an intuitive life means trusting your true values and being able to rely entirely on yourself.

Especially in these times when we are exposed to so much fake news and manipulations every day, it is more important than ever to be able to rely on yourself completely.

We benefit from communicating with our souls. It means we realize that we are the creator of our own lives and that no one can influence or manipulate us to our disadvantage.

We have the gut feeling we talk about, which is our second brain. There is a lot of scientific research regarding this topic. Trust your feelings by understanding that your gut is your second brain. A big part of our emotional and mental system is reflected in our guts. It is the one thing that we have forgotten: intuition.

Each of us knows this feeling that something is not right without really being able to explain it.

However, we are no longer used to listening to our intuition in our perfect world. Instead, we are conditioned to receive all information from a foreign, artificial source. As a result, we put the mind over the heart and disconnect ourselves from our true nature.

When something is so perfect, if a person is so perfect in a perfect relationship, or if a job is so perfect or whatever, we don't want to destroy it by our intuition. Yet, our intuition is the only thing we should listen to because it's not about perfection; it's about following your heart and trusting life instead of trusting algorithms.

Many people are drawn to this specific construct when something is beautiful on the outside.

They believe that it is, therefore, essential to them. By believing in this matrix, you forget that your intuition would tell you what is going on behind this perfect construct and what is good or bad for you.

Based on your beliefs of this matrix, you will not rely on your intuition, even if you feel it deep inside. I am not telling anyone to attend more seminars or to search for another journey or whatever most of you have experienced on this quest. I am telling you one very simple thing.

Even if you are interested in learning how to channel and enhance your intuition to its highest form, the Lovetuner will always do one thing for you in any case: it will get you talking to your gut and your heart.

Our gut feeling is also vibrational energy. When you understand that harmony is reflected in every cell of your body, when something harmonizes with you, then you will understand that it is very wise to listen to your gut feeling; no matter what the projection of the matrix, which anyways only tricks you, tells your brain.

The real art of channeling is not for seeking answers, is not for seeking a new way, is not for searching for a new path in life. The real form of intuition and channeling is to reconnect to your soul and feel that you have come here as an eternal being with a divine purpose.

In the next step, you reconnect to your compatible energy and become whole again. Finally, you will feel you are here because you planned it and have a purpose.

You will discover that you are here to follow your vision rather than other people's ideas and rules. You are born to discover the secrets of life on your terms.

Then, when you start to improve your intuition, when you start to channel, you will see the unseen, explore the unexplored, and stop searching. You will no longer look for the way.

You will understand, and you will be able to live it in the consequence that you are the way, you are the light, you are the divine, and you are the love. You are all that is, and all that is you.

Channeling does not mean that you have to answer other people's questions.

Channeling itself is the answer to all the questions in this universe because you are the universe.

You are the essence of life; you are everything that is; you are the divine essence of the universe. If you keep on channeling for quite some time, you will eventually merge entirely with your divine compatible energy.

It will improve life in any given way to the extent that your mind cannot imagine. It will get you to a point where you will no longer accept anything that is not authentic and in alignment with yourself. You will only accept the best, the highest, and the most divine for yourself and mankind.

CHAPTER XV

FROM A PHYSICAL TO A VIBRATIONAL BEING

For more than 30 years, we have been in a turbulent transformation phase, the so-called Ascension Process of our planet. We, as a whole humanity, experience the light-body process within the ascension process.

Numerous cosmic events that support humans and planet Earth in our ascension from the fourth into the fifth dimension are occurring. It is a purification process for both the earth and humanity.

Our entire solar system is entering a multi-star system. As a result, planet Earth is transforming to a higher dimension, and humanity will create an entirely new system of coexistence.

In this transitional period, we all can break out of rigid patterns, evolve in harmony with nature, transform ego-driven behavior, and manifest unconditional love for everything in existence. The cosmic influences are right on target with the prevailing attitude of the respectful mind.

External events trigger internal action processes. Physical sensitivities can arise while we transform old imprints and programs and thereby dissolve old patterns, behaviors, and blockages.

The dense matter is increasingly lightened by cosmic radiation, becoming lighter and vibrating higher. The entire cell system of the human being is subject to a change, which ultimately also changes and upgrades the DNA.

The cells of all living beings store light, and the totality of this light controls the life processes.

Every cell in everybody is allowed to adapt to the new vibration of the earth. As a result, the collective consciousness will rise to a higher level of consciousness.

The awakening of a new humanity that respects all that is acts for the benefit of all that is and recognizes and accepts that its creative power represents the next stage of evolution. Our future is the effect of the causes we set now.

Due to the increased vibrational frequency of the earth, everything pulsates and vibrates faster, including human beings. Consequently, also time experiences an acceleration.

Time is an instrument of the third dimension, so dual experiences are possible. Already in the fourth dimension, we leave the usual time structure and find that everything, negative and positive, manifests itself immediately. Our soul cycle uses time to move from experience to experience and from life to life. Time separates everything. Duality can only be explored through separation from unity. On the human journey of evolvement and discovery, the linear timeline offers the opportunity to realize that ultimately all things are interacting, everything is interconnected, and is One Journey.

The goal of the soul's incarnational cycle is to explore all experiences on the linear timeline and then take the journey back to the source.

During the global transformation process, time accelerates more and more, finally imploding. In higher dimensions, we experience time as a factor that is expandable. In higher consciousness, we can expand time infinitely and thus create space for ourselves within infinity.

In cosmic consciousness, only the moment counts, the presence at the moment, or the here and now. Several time levels exist simultaneously, side by side, whose reality levels are separated only by the different vibration frequencies.

Spiritual time travel is possible in higher dimensions, and the transition from dimension to dimension does not appear abstract but logical. It is experienced as a presence of being. A brief look into old material about the ascension process reveals that the light-body process is a cosmic cycle that is fulfilled with the transformation into the fifth dimension. Every single step of the 12 stages of the light-body process is not linear but multidimensional and works through simultaneous integration work.

How quickly, extensively, and intensively such a transformation process proceeds depends on the overall position of the individual or being.

Each soul of an individual represents a unique composition of light and sound within the cosmos. Every human being, every living being, has differentiated experiences that differ in intensity and frequency—each one is individual in its own way and embodies a unique cosmic fingerprint.

The 12 light-body process steps are, therefore, to be understood as a schematic model. In this book, I want to point out the most critical steps.

The Lovetuner massively supports this transformation, which is not always a so-called walk in the park, and tuning can help you to always stay in the state of unconditional love in your heart.

This can make your transformation process faster and easier in any way.

Level 1:

The mutations begin in the brain at the interface between the mental and physical bodies. The electrochemical and electromagnetic processes and conditions change.

Level 2:

Telepathic contact with familiar people become more frequent. Messages from higher levels are received. Likewise, manifestations of nonlinear thinking occur more frequently. The mind begins to understand that there are higher levels of guidance and begins to cooperate with the higher self to gain a better understanding and a greater overview.

Level 3:

The physical body transforms low-vibrational energy into higher-vibrational light energy in its metabolism. The light absorbed by the small vortices (fulcrums) on the skin's surface reaches corresponding vortices in the cells inside the body. The mitochondria, the power plants of the cells, absorb the light as food and produce more adenosine triphosphate. ATP is the only and immediately available energy carrier in the cell and an essential regulator for energy-providing processes.

Level 4:

The transformation in the area of the interface between the mental body and the physical body in the brain continues. The electrochemical and electromagnetic processes are changing again.

Nerve connections in the brain are restructured, affecting the sense of sight and hearing, among other things, and new brain functions are activated. This includes the synchronization of the two hemispheres of the brain. For many people, very unfamiliar experiences in multidimensional thinking can arise.

Level 5:

Telepathic contacts with familiar people accumulate again, and more contents from higher levels come through. The mental body, the carrier of the mind, begins to make the first changes in its previous beliefs based on its experiences of three-dimensionality. The mind begins to understand that guidance is being created at higher levels, providing a more multidimensional overview of daily life.

Level 6:

The person is now increasingly growing into the consciousness of their multidimensional being.

Traditional beliefs turn out to be dogmas or dissolve. Other people with similar experiences increasingly enter our lives.

Whoever masters this sixth stage can expect that their old identity will largely dissolve and that they will find their way to a more mature personality. As in the third stage, other parts of the soul descend and gradually integrate.

This process is undoubtedly one of the most difficult things to endure. Many, who have reached their breaking point here, decide to leave their bodies to complete their light-body process in later life.

Level 7:

Revolutionary emotional processes characterize this phase; they are dissolving one after another, especially those patterns associated with ideas of worthlessness, incompetence, shame, and guilt. Intense mood swings often accompany this, and tearful outbursts of joy may be replaced by periods of sadness and fits of anger.

In addition, the heart chakra opens with an unprecedented intensity: the old seal dissolves, and our heart center begins to transform into a dimensional gateway again.

Finally, the mental body begins to mature to increase focus on the here and now. When a person reaches this stage, they can appear quite cold to others because they can no longer establish low- vibrational emotional interactions.

Being stuck in old behavioral patterns is the reason for certain beliefs, such as the "criminals in politics" and "bad people" in general. Next to the third eye, the space of the pineal gland, the so-called fourth eye develops in the parietal area near the fontanel, the sense organ for multidimensional vision.

Once the pineal gland has grown to its full size, it begins to work as intended, and the entire inner glandular system is transformed. The consequence, in the course of the seventh stage, is the aging process turns around and the entire organism rejuvenates.

Facial expressions and wrinkles change. At this stage, it is possible that we suddenly receive a connection to other aspects of our soul as part of our divine self, and we can look through our multidimensional eyes into a multidimensional reality. At this point, it is essential to explicitly point out the following:

The characteristics of this seventh stage can often be spiritual arrogance. Spiritual arrogance is one of the most insidious traps we can experience on the path of spiritual evolution. Sooner or later, we all get concerned.

What matters is how you deal with it. Realizing that the true master knows he is not a master can help to overcome this level and provide comfort in times of confusion when we are not yet fully able to let go of selfish motivations.

Are you ignoring divine humility? Or are you aware that we are learning more every day? If you lose sight of yourself and the ability to be a disciple because you are too busy being a master or a guru for others, then only an honest reflection on the fact that stagnation is the death of any development will help.

The only look that helps you look forward is looking back at yourself and your behavior.

Whoever claims to be anything has completed his development at this moment because he defines his state of being as absolute.

During our life we accumulate a lot of knowledge, and we think we understand a lot. However, knowledge only means taking in information. This does not say anything about whether we have understood this information. You surely know that is the point where knowledge becomes cognition.

Only then have we understood the information. That's why sometimes we read or hear certain content in 20 different forms, and only at the twenty-first time do we read or hear it in such a way that it clicks, and we understand that this is what the other 20 times have already trying to tell us. So, the knowledge in the heart has become wisdom.

You can see spiritual arrogance, in fact, when it is difficult for you to accept criticism, when you have the feeling that you have to defend your point of view in any case, or have the feeling inside that you look down on the other person from above because you know more, are further, experience or perceive things more intensively.

Always pay attention to the feeling of true divine humility. If you think you already know everything, then it is time to pause. If you think you cannot learn anything from your teachers or others or that you are better than them, then it is time to acknowledge that a change of consciousness or a realization on your part is needed. Nothing matters; opinions are like this today and will be changed tomorrow. They are just the gossip of yesterday.

The Lovetuner supports a humble, genuine insight. Tuning can help you develop your heart center instead of losing yourself in spiritual arrogance. Be aware that the true masters have always remained disciples.

Some more pearls of wisdom along the way:

Spiritual arrogance is gaining an ability, which one wished for so long that it became obsolete.

"The fool says what he knows, the wise man knows what he says." — Jewish proverb.

"I know that I know nothing." — Socrates / Goethe.

Learn to read in your heart rather than in the books of this world, for in the books of this world you read only what others have found in their hearts.

Level 8:

Changes in the quality of partnerships take place. The longing for a partner with a harmonious vibrational behavior becomes evident.

Unequal partnerships are dissolved, and the sexual need of the conventional kind decreases clearly.

Preference is given to acts of merging that involve the entire being or the entire field of light.

Such fusions, which lead to cosmic orgasms, are only possible between partners whose vibrational signature is very similar.

Level 9:

The multidimensional self becomes a daily reality, and the full potential to manifest it on the physical level becomes subjective. We experience that we are increasingly expressing the high divine qualities of divine will and divine power, divine light, divine love, and divine truth.

Levels 10–12:

Levels ten through twelve are called the "spiritual levels." The lower four bodies are fused into one energy field, and the higher chakras are completely connected to the oversoul or the web of love.

We now largely correspond to the fully developed galactic human being; we have abilities that are part of our ancestral heritage.

In the future, when most people have reached the eleventh light-body stage, a mass potential will have been reached whose high vibration and frequency transcends the previous space-time structure.

At the twelfth level, the person strives for perfection as a true galactic being. All abilities and qualities fully blossom, and those chosen to serve on earth are now fully involved in reorganizing all human and earthly affairs.

It is the spiritual mission of the Lovetuner. I am fully dedicated to fulfilling this mission in any given way to overcome all boundaries and connect and unite all hearts. Therefore, I have studied the knowledge of the divine laws to get insight into the divine plan to act with full responsibility, and I want to share my knowledge with you.

This is the future we are all creating together:

one world - one love - one tone

All humans will settle into the now-reached fifth dimension and develop an entirely new relationship of consciousness with Mother Earth.

A new humanity has blossomed, fulfilling its responsibilities as a galactic sentinel civilization to both Gaia and the Galactic Federation of Light. Humanity is resuming its galactic heritage, connecting heaven with earth and being closer to the Creator than ever before. Now humanity has come of age. The matrix is switched off from all sides; that is quantum evolution. From below when the crystalline heart of Gaia ignites from its core. From above, cosmically and with the help of our intergalactic allies. Through us from within, as we awaken and break out of the frequency of the matrix, DNA upgrades, more strands are unlocked, triggered by the higher frequencies.

In turn, our energetic flow, our chakra system, will be fully activated. We are experiencing many symptoms of this accelerated cosmic recalibration.

Every wave we surf now lifts us into higher frequency fields; this wave is unstoppable and gets better and faster. This is because the universal spectrum of frequencies is broad and multidimensional.

The matrix works in a very small space on the lower frequencies of the cosmic spectrum of life.

We are being elevated, some of us are even catapulted as soon as the readiness is conscious and openly communicated. For it has long since been decided.

Each tidal wave pushes and pulls us to expand and energetically release, recalibrate, adjust, redeem, and constantly connect to the universal love frequency, the 528 Hz frequency.

We are experiencing an intense karmic evolution that exists for the first time in this explicit form, and that is completely transforming all of humanity. We are experiencing this on an unprecedented scale of surpassing all-encompassing love and goodness. This transition is being accelerated because it is overdue on planet Earth, and from now on only something better will follow.

Many say we are behind schedule. Yet any good schedule includes space to integrate upgrades and recalibrate outdated operations. As a result, we may be in a cosmic waiting room, a kind of space held in time to allow us to change ourselves and our world completely and permanently.

This, indeed, is a challenging task. From ground zero on earth, the trenches of the front lines, life is pushed up week after week. The weather and the seasons are unpredictable; time fluctuates, and there is no longer a so-called normalcy because the new wants to be born naturally out into the world. As the matrix dissolves, its agenda of rules and retribution, revenge, mind control algorithms, and predatory programming completely collapses. Awakened people change the field of the matrix.

When we awaken, we become obvious disturbances in the previous matrix. We no longer mindlessly submit to the conditioning, the imposed control system, the unjust machinations, the senseless pressure to conform, and the fear of retribution.

The camouflage mode practiced by many awakened ones, star seeders, and light workers since their birth here is finally being shed, like a snake shedding its skin.

More and more people are online and anchoring their light into Gaia's grid of evolved crystalline light. We anchor into higher frequencies to establish, correlate, and complement Gaia's ascension into the frequency spectrum.

Go inside and simplify your life. There is so much going on that many may feel like rabbits caught in the headlights.

At the same time, they are horrified by the current state of the world and delighted at how beautiful the human experience can be on Gaia.

We move up and down in the frequency spectrum, pinballs in a cosmic arcade game. The centering of ourselves balances us and helps us regain balance to act consciously with the collected power in a new direction. The merging of our whole selves is a profound transition that will sometimes be a little difficult, but it is definitely worth it, so hang in there!

Inner calmness brings outer peace. Go within for serenity and simplify your life for outer peace.

Preserve your strength and personal space in the coming time; you will need it. We will be pushed back to the core of our being to blossom and bear fruit in full splendor in a completely new, authentically adequate, sincere, wonderful, and authentic way.

Earth Warriors, Light Warriors, Light Bearers, and Keepers of the Light have long been successfully active in the background so far unnoticed. From now on, the light will reveal itself faster and faster and more and more. So do not worry but go forward with courage despite your fearful head.

Light workers are alive, present, and connected to this wondrous world at this momentous time in its evolution. Be yourself as authentically as possible, and if you are not sure who that is, find out for real. We are the change we want to see in the world.

Accept, tune, help, and meditate. Meditate, even if it is uncomfortable for others, and do not be ashamed to accept help or necessary coaching. Name selfish politics, fascist or condescending rhetoric, unfriendly language, negative mean thoughts, degrading beliefs, and exploitative systems and challenge them to change or get out of the toxic system now. Do this from your pure whole heart and with clearly benevolent intent in the sense of the realization of human dignity and the realized good for all at the same time. Breathe deeply into the ebb and flow of the cosmic surfing that uplifts us. Listen carefully to your innermost true being, which has the best intentions for all beings, and react immediately to the wisdom of your proactive benevolent intuition.

Take the best possible care of yourself. Practice self-care, and reprogram yourself with daily guided meditations, visualizations, mantras, rest periods, healing therapies, conscious alignment, and mindfulness such as love tuning. Step as often as you can into the frequencies of gratitude, joy, and love in an uplifting way, thereby consciously raising your frequency.

Be a role model, guide others out of their distress, and do something meaningfully good because it raises you simultaneously. Unless you do it to distract yourself, then finally take care of yourself first; otherwise, you can never help people with full force to fulfilling independence.

Be kind to yourself, protect yourself, and welcome a change in your friendship relations. Be happy for others as if it had just happened to you and succeeded. We are creating the new Earth now accelerating and strengthening, integrating, and reconnecting with Gaia; we are in the middle of an intense change and recalibration.

Be good to yourself! Remain on this surfboard to the highest degree, ride the waves to higher frequencies, in love and light-filled turning, sending it inward and outward.

One more word about "healing" and "healer":

Many people want to heal. All kinds of things are offered today, starting with "chakra healing", "karma healing," "aura balancing," and much more.

Please consider that the person who is working in your system has direct access, i.e., influence on your physical body and also on your subtle bodies.

The healer is not always aware of this. Many jump on this train, not for the sake of healing, but because it is hip at this time to deal with alternative healing methods. In this case, the spiritual world wants us to be aware that the most important thing is to heal ourselves before reaching out to others.

Without precise knowledge of what is happening on the level of subtle energies, healing can be a rather dangerous business, not least because it can be wrong to heal a specific person under certain circumstances. There are diseases and life situations which are karmic. conditioned learning processes which one has to work through to remove karma.

Furthermore, one may only heal when asked to do so. People seek help from someone powerful in healing; this is only natural. In any case, it is wrong for a healer, on their own initiative, to seek people to heal. Healing before the chakras are properly opened will affect your own body.

The healer can then not see when another person needs help. For example, in the case of a closed heart center, the cosmic green cannot come through. Instead, the healer must go back to their ethereal green and supply from this.

In many cases, the heart is the most challenging region to open. For this reason, many healers have died of heart failure. When the energies hit a closed heart center during healing, this is felt as a strike in the heart and may manifest as a mild heart attack.

In a closed throat chakra, the energies will cause throat diseases and colds, in which case it is more than doubtful to be a good healer. A closed third-eye chakra destroys all healing powers anyway.

Let us take a look at the bright side.

It is your task to be a role model and human companion for people who, like you, will experience the journey from the old to the new energy. The path you are taking now will enable you to have experiences that will enable you to be the ambassador for the spiritual world and helper for others in the future.

Always be aware: As exhausting as your journey to the inside can be from time to time, you are never alone. All these symptoms will pass. You are a creator, and you are now a channel of the divine, and you are gaining in love, trust, and quality of life. You are an ambassador for the spiritual world.

At any time, you can and may ask for help and support from the spiritual world. Swift and practical help is also the so-called "light bow" or "arc work," a method developed and registered by Anne Wolnik, and separation work, or repatriation, to dissolve the symptoms and causes.

You are not alone, we are all one big community, and it is our task to put our service into the service of humanity. In doing so, we do not have to suffer, but may be happy and experience the fullness of being.

Let us help you and be aware. Ascension cannot be reached within three days. It is a process that brings you love, knowledge, fullness, understanding of being, and great fulfillment.

CHAPTER XVI

LOVETUNER AND THE VISION FOR THE FUTURE OF MANKIND

It is essential to understand that the world we live in is not a human society. Our society is killing authenticity. Whatever makes you real, whatever is authentic, is getting eliminated by our society.

Very little in our society helps you heal; it is even worse that it undermines what we consider healing or what we consider a whole and authentic human being. Society likes you to be addicted to whatever this manufactured creation wants you to be. It wants you to have the feeling of being not whole, to have the feeling of being inadequate.

Whatever you are trying to accomplish, first, you need to find your vibration, and then you will see that is not aligned with what society expects from you or what people's expectations are for you. It has nothing to do with you; it's like there is no love in this whole thing, and if you try to fit in, you are denying yourself and you are accepting a completely fake construct, a fake society.

Instead of being your true self, you are living in a culture that kills exactly this. It is where we all need to awaken our higher self, be beyond the point of judgment, and not feel guilty about not fulfilling society's expectations. Society is fake anyways, and the only truth you have is yourself.

You will find all answers within you when you connect to your heart.

That's why the Lovetuner makes it easy to find your core resonance. Of course, as individuals, we can pick up and point out what is not appropriate in our society, but if we want to heal, as a society, and as humanity, then we need to connect heart to heart.

There is no fakeness in the heart; this is all a created matrix. What we need to do is to be authentic. Authenticity is the path to wholeness. This path towards wholeness we can create as a collective; we can support each other to overcome what our culture and society have undermined for so long.

We can take it on for ourselves as an individuals, but also, most importantly, do it as a collective to awaken other hearts. Tuning in means touching and healing one heart at a time and connecting hearts one after the other. It is the only way you can overcome the programming and the propaganda that society did or is still doing.The frequency of your soul is pure light, and when you align this with the 528 Hz frequency when you tune in, you overcome dissonance and experience freedom on a cellular level, and then all makes sense.

As we cannot change anything from the outside, the change must come from within. When we start this process, this overriding and reprogramming can happen.

It is the future of humanity, and this is the future of every individual; love is the answer. It is what we are supposed to feel, and what we are supposed to send out into the universe: love and light.

All is one and one is all.

The Lovetuner Foundation

Launching the Lovetuner Foundation was one of my most important tasks. In the following, I would like to share my motivations for this with you.

The Lovetuner Foundation is a California-based nonprofit organization with the mission to empower individuals and communities to heal through breath, frequency, and vibration. The Foundation's purpose is to bring the healing power of mindfulness meditation through the combination of breathwork and the 528 Hz frequency to people of all ages and, in particular, to those who would otherwise not have access.

The Lovetuner Foundation's historical focus has been in the educational sector, striving to inspire mindfulness in the next generation. We believe that the next generation is the source of change in our society. By incorporating mindfulness and meditation at a young age, we can teach self-empowerment, emotional control, and compassion for others.

In 2014, Lovetuner first began working in the schools and, in 2018, joined Pure Edge, a nonprofit organization focusing on health and well-being in the education system. As a result, over 50,000 teachers and students have integrated Lovetuner practice into their school day, bringing calm and clarity to the classroom, which enhances academic learning, creates a marked re-education in bullying and school violence, and provides meaningful support for socio-emotional learning (SEL) and the development of important life skills.

Based on this success in the schools, the Lovetuner Foundation began working with veteran programs to help heal the scars of war and provide a drug-free solution to combat the effects of PTSD. The Lovetuner is also effective in suicide prevention and helping maintain mental health, and has also been shown to increase employee satisfaction, improve communication, and increase productivity by bringing a mindfulness approach to the corporate sector.

The Lovetuner Foundation teams up with Lovetuner and the Lovetuner team riders, exceptional individuals from various fields and backgrounds who all share our mission to make this world a happier, healthier, more peaceful and unified place, and to bring to life the Lovetuner mindfulness programs.

These programs teach people how to empower themselves and enter into a frequency where they resonate with positivity. The Lovetuner is the tool that combines breathwork and sound healing. The simple breathing exercise that is done with the Lovetuner connects you to the 528 Hz frequency. The 528 Hz frequency is one of the significant solfeggio healing frequencies.

As you use the Lovetuner, your breath connects you to the 528 Hz frequency, which works on a cellular level to put you into a state of deep relaxation. In this state, you can relieve anxiety, reduce stress, work through trauma, enter a positive mindset, and resonate on a higher frequency.

The Lovetuner mindfulness programs have the power to change lives. Individuals walk away with a new outlook on life and with the tool to help them overcome obstacles and break down barriers.

The mission of the Lovetuner Foundation is to make the healing power of the Lovetuner available to everyone. The Lovetuner is more than a product, it is a peace and love mission, and the Lovetuner Foundation is the tool that makes it possible to make this healing tool available to everyone and to facilitate life-changing programs for those who might experience hardship in accessing such a program.

We welcome you to join us on our mission to create a revolutionary change on our planet through vibration and frequency. Your donation can make a difference.

The Lovetuner and an Act of Kindness

As the saying goes: "In a world where you can be anything, be kind." I would love to introduce you to our act of kindness.

What is an act of kindness?

An act of kindness is when you make a sacrifice to help others without expecting anything in return. Most often, an act of kindness is performed by a stranger or someone you don't know well.

The Lovetuner organization started with a mission to help create a better world. With our goal in mind, we accept an act of kindness as a currency for a Lovetuner. If you or someone you know has completed an act of kindness that has changed lives, we are happy to accept your act of kindness in exchange for a Lovetuner, as long as it aligns with our guidelines.

Kindness is a superpower and one that can create amazing and lasting change.

The Lovetuner Community

The Lovetuner mission has become a worldwide movement and created a global community.

Every day we are told that people from all over the world are tuning alone or participating in powerful group tunings. This positive feedback touches our hearts and makes us humble and ever-grateful!

CHAPTER XVII

GRATITUDE

When we talk about frequency and vibration, we acknowledge a frequency hierarchy.

Gratitude is a very high frequency. Gratitude can help you to be happy with the life you are living.

Gratitude is not just the feeling of being grateful for what good things have happened to you or the circumstances in which you live, but also for accepting and being at peace with the not-so-good things that happen in life.

Genuine gratitude is accepting life as a whole, not just for the little things that please us. It is not cherry-picking only the best. When you practice gratitude, life begins to make sense, even for the past that has happened, and it gives you peace in the here and now.

It also gives us a vision for the future.

Being grateful for where you have come from, where you are right now, and where you are going opens a different perspective on life and makes you humble.

Also, gratitude is a very healthy human emotion. The more you consciously express gratitude for what you have, the more you will receive. Therefore, gratitude will expand. That is the beauty of gratitude. That is why it is such a powerful and healing emotion.

When you fully understand gratitude, it can unlock the wholeness of your life. It transforms what we are and what we have into enough; more than that, it transforms denial into acceptance.

It transforms chaos into order and gives us clarity. It is the end of confusion because you understand at a deep cellular level that gratitude transforms everything into enough.

The Lovetuner gives you easy access to any emotion, any frequency you want to connect with.

When you do the breathing exercise with the Lovetuner, it automatically aligns your cellular structure; it gives you the feeling of relaxation.

Especially when it comes to gratitude, this is something I recommend doing: consciously tune into what you are grateful for. The 528 Hz frequency will enhance that feeling in you; as I said before, gratitude always creates more.

On the one hand, you understand that what you are and what you have is already enough. But as you go further, it brings more gratitude because your life experiences become more beautiful and satisfying. Connecting with nature and seeing the little things is extremely important regarding gratitude. The Lovetuner with this cosmic frequency or miracle frequency of 528 Hz helps you build a solid and powerful connection with nature.

After tuning for a while, you will understand that subconsciously your entire being gets more aligned with Mother Nature, and you have a stronger connection. When you embrace nature and you are grateful for it, this is where healing starts and where expansion starts.

What you should do, what we all can do, is make the conscious choice to be grateful and, most importantly, to embrace the wholeness of life with an attitude of gratitude.

BIBLIOGRAPHY

HeartMath Institute. (2011). You Can Change Your DNA. Articles of the heart/ personal development, pp. 21-23.

Mind Vibrations.com. (2020). 528 Hz DNA Repair – A Guide to the Science & Benefits, pp. 22.

Lipton, B. (2017), The Jump from Cell Culture to Consciousness. Integrative Medicine: A Clinician´s Journal, pp. 61.

Royal Rife Machines (2020). Royal Rife Frequency Machines FAQ., pp. 64.

Babayi, T, R. G. (2017). The Effects of 528 Hz Sound Wave to Reduce Cell Death in Human Astrocyte Primary Cell Culture Treated with Ethanol. Journal of Addiction Research & Therapy, pp. 65.

Gimzewski, James K. (2020). University of Southern California, pp. 65.

Lorenzen, D. L. (n.d.). The Story of Clustered Water. Engineered Lifestyles, pp. 66.

Hulce, D. D. (2009). An Inspiring Journey of how Ancient Solfeggio Frequencies are Empowering Personal and Planetary Evolution. A Fork in the Road, pp. 67.

Dodge, Heather (2010) Miracle in the Gulf of Mexico. OpEd News Journal, pp. 67.

Saykally, R. J. (2001). The SayKally Group, University of Berkeley, California, pp. 67.

Kaho Akimoto, H. K. (2018). The Effect of 528 Hz Music on the Endocrine and the Autonomic Nervous System. Tokyo, Japan: Jujendo Graduate School of Medicine, pp.74.

Horowitz, D. L. (2019). The 528 Hz Frequency. The Book of 528: Prosperity Key of Love. Medical Veritas International Inc., pp. 80-85.

Morgan, S. J. M. (2017). Effect of Heart Rate Variability Biofeedback on Sport Performance. National Library of Medicine, pp. 106-107.

Luskin, Frederic P., Reitz, Megan, B., & al, e. (2002). A Controlled Pilot Study of Stress. Preventive Cardiology, University of Stanford, pp. 107.

Hurst, K. (2019). 7 Hermetic Principles: Laws Of The Universe According To The Kybalion, pp. 123-124.

ACKNOWLEDGEMENTS

First and foremost I would like to thank my two kids, Adina and Luis, and my dear friend and co-author Anne for supporting me and motivating me to write this book. Also, I would like to say thank you to the global Lovetuner community for your consistent support that makes it possible to share my mission and create a positive shift of consciousness in this world which allows humanity to get from dissonance into resonance. I would also like to say thank you to all our Lovetuner advocates and team riders for integrating the Lovetuner into their work and spreading the love.

I am honored that my two beloved children possess an understanding of the necessity of mindfulness at their young age. I would like to share with you their thoughts and experience with the Lovetuner and the impact this mission has had on them. It makes me feel humble to see their dedication and unconditional love.

One Love,
Sigmar

MESSAGE
BY ADINA BERG

I first heard about the Lovetuner through snippets of conversation with my dad. Like most preteen girls, I wasn't very invested in what I saw as my dad's next project. I always saw my dad as a highly intelligent person, someone who had a wealth of information stored in his mind, surprising you with intriguing facts.

Naturally, when he talked about the Lovetuner and went into details about the 528 Hz frequency, it piqued my curiosity. Yet, it wasn't until I tried the Lovetuner for myself that I became fully aware of the power this small tool possessed. Our family stood in a circle outside, my dad explaining the simple exercise: "Take a deep breath, and gently exhale, allowing your breath to create a steady tone. Try to hold your exhale for as long as you can," he encouraged.

We would start with six cycles. We all placed the Lovetuners between our lips. Air flowed through my nostrils, flooding my lungs. Once filled with air, I began to exhale. Slowly letting the air escape me as a beautiful soothing sound met my ears. I had heard the tone before, each time my dad was tuning nearby, but this time I felt it vibrating through my whole body. As I released my second breath, my ears perked up to the alluring sound being created by the combination of multiple people tuning.

Although none of us were moving, I could feel us becoming physically closer, our bond to one another strengthening. Nine years later, I still get this feeling each time I tune in with a group of people. No matter the size of the group or our connection previous to that moment, I can feel the link between us being nourished.

The Lovetuner brings me a compelling feeling of unity. The power I feel within my own breath when using the Lovetuner revitalizes my entire mind, body, and spirit. As the years have passed, the Lovetuner has become a fundamental part of my life. I sometimes take for granted how lucky I am to have gotten access to such a powerful tool at an early age.

Any time I felt anxious, stressed, sad, angry, or just needed a reset, the Lovetuner was there, hanging around my neck. I never had to be taught how to calm myself down or clear my mind of negative thoughts; the Lovetuner made it come naturally. Before a test, as I watched my classmates around me scrambling, trying to cram the last bit of information into their brains, I would simply close my eyes, grab my Lovetuner and do six breathing cycles. Before every race, whether it be running or swimming, I took a moment during my warm-up

stretches to reconnect with myself using the Lovetuner.
I visualized my energy coursing through my body with each long exhale. The Lovetuner gave me confidence in myself. It reassured me that I possessed the power to take control and that I was capable of anything I set my mind, soul, and body to. Each day I am grateful that I was handed this tool. In the morning, when I wake up, putting the tuner to my lips before I even have a sip of water, I am setting a positive intention. I begin each day using my breath, combining it with the 528 Hz frequency, reminding myself of the power that lies within me. I believe that everyone on this planet deserves to experience this feeling. The Lovetuner is the tool that can make you recognize your potential and the strength you own.

The Lovetuner is the tool that is changing the world because it reconnects people back to their spirit. In a world of polarization and disjointedness, the most important thing is to harness the power of unity and to remind yourself that we are all connected. We all are powerful, and it is up to you to harness your potential.

Adina Berg

MESSAGE
BY LUIS BERG

I have been tuning for many years now.

It has been the easiest and fastest way for me to become calm and connected. Within minutes I am relaxed and focused. It's improved every aspect of my life; in school, I have noticed since elementary when my whole class would tune.

We all got better scores on tests and quizzes. I used the Lovetuner before sports, and I was able to zone out of everything else in my life and focus on the game. I kept tuning before tests through middle school, high school, and now college.

It took the nerves away and allowed me to be more confident and decisive. And tuning not only helps me with stressful situations like tests or sports, but when I am tired, it gives me energy, and when I can't unwind, or I'm frustrated or just want to take some time to go within myself.

A few minutes of tuning relieves all of those feelings, allowing me to approach everything with a clear mind. A couple of years ago when my parents got divorced and my sister and I decided to live with my dad, the Lovetuner gave me comfort, and I started using my Lovetuner much more.

It allowed me to get through those difficult times in my life, gaining a routine and improving my mental and physical health. And I think the Lovetuner can help everyone in those difficult times because it gives you the inner strength to face those challenges when nothing else seems to help.

Instead of numbing yourself to avoid the feeling you have, empower yourself and choose how you feel.

Luis Berg

Luis Berg, Sigmar Berg, Adina Berg

Made in the USA
Las Vegas, NV
08 November 2024

11319206R00105